12/20

"Twenty-volume folios
will never make a revolution.
It's the little pocket pamphlets
that are to be feared."
Voltaire

FIELD (#1) NOTES

MARK KINGWELL

On Risk

Or, If You Play, You Pay: The Politics

of Chance in a Plague Year

BIBLIOASIS

Windsor, Ontario

FIRST EDITION

Library and Archives Canada Cataloguing in Publication

Title: On risk, or, If you play, you pay : the politics of chance in a plague year /
Mark Kingwell.
Other titles: If you play, you pay
Names: Kingwell, Mark, 1963- author.
Description: Series statement: Field notes ; 1 | Includes bibliographical
references.
Identifiers: Canadiana (print) 20200303376 | Canadiana (ebook)
20200303635 | ISBN 9781771963923
   (softcover) | ISBN 9781771963930 (ebook)
Subjects: LCSH: Risk—Sociological aspects. | LCSH: Risk—Political aspects. |
LCSH: Death. | LCSH:
   COVID-19 (Disease)—Social aspects. | LCSH: COVID-19 (Disease)—Political
aspects. | LCSH:
   Epidemics—Social aspects. | LCSH: Epidemics—Political aspects.
Classification: LCC HM1101 .K56 2020 | DDC 302/.12—dc23

Edited by Daniel Wells
Copyedited by John Sweet
Typeset by Vanessa Stauffer
Series designed by Ingrid Paulson

Published with the generous assistance of the Canada Council for the Arts,
which last year invested $153 million to bring the arts to Canadians throughout
the country, and the financial support of the Government of Canada. Biblioasis
also acknowledges the support of the Ontario Arts Council (OAC), an agency of
the Government of Ontario, which last year funded 1,709 individual artists
and 1,078 organizations in 204 communities across Ontario, for a total of
$52.1 million, and the contribution of the Government of Ontario through the
Ontario Book Publishing Tax Credit and Ontario Creates.

PRINTED AND BOUND IN CANADA

Contents

I liked Mr. Josie's face very much ... [I]t was a face that had not been sculptured for a quick or facile success. It had been formed at sea, on the profitable side of bars, playing cards with other gamblers, and by enterprises of great risk conceived and undertaken with cold and exact intelligence.

Ernest Hemingway, "Pursuit as Happiness" (2008)*

....

* A previously unpublished story about marlin fishing, drinking, and defeat. Ernest Hemingway, "Pursuit as Happiness," *New Yorker*, June 1, 2020.

Preface: The Plague Years

IF YOU PLAY, you pay—a simple truth. But some pay more than others, and a lot of the time, past winners keep on winning. Risk is theoretically neutral and indifferent, an exercise of pure randomness. But, as the 2020 pandemic has shown us, when natural forces meet social and cultural conditions, risk can get redistributed very fast. We're not really all in this together. The eternal human story is that some people win, others lose, and often the first is true only because the second is likewise. The current realities have offered a forced education in the politics of risk, a bleak tutorial on taking chances.

Education is, all by itself, what Gert Biesta calls "a beautiful risk"—lighting a fire, not filling a bucket, as Yeats said.* Socrates, that risk-taker in the service of education, understood the risks all too well. In Plato's *Phaedo*,

....

* Gert J.J. Biesta, *The Beautiful Risk of Education* (Boulder, CO: Paradigm, 2013).

Socrates drinks the hemlock decreed for those convicted of corrupting youth and praising false gods, and reminds his friend and neighbour Crito to sacrifice a rooster to Asklepios, son of Apollo and a divine healer. This is not because Socrates wants to be resurrected—a power that Asklepios was thought to have—but because he wanted to acknowledge his debt to the release of the soul from the body's prison that comes with death. (The scene was depicted heroically in 1787 by the French neoclassical painter Jacques-Louis David, with a very buff Socrates pointing to the heavens and reaching for the poisoned chalice, as Plato is bowed in mourning at the foot of his bed.) We moderns don't usually have the same view of death, or of the soul, or even of education. But we face the same mortal challenges.[*]

An old saying, sometimes attributed to Cicero, says this: "To philosophize is to learn how to die." You may be wondering: What could this mean? Start with what it doesn't mean. Learning how to die does not mean that philosophy is a kind of nihilistic death cult, a sort of cabal of necronauts with one foot in the grave and the other on a metaphysical banana peel. True, we philosophers are perfectly capable of doubting the existence of rocks and trees, or believing that this entire ceremony is a simulation in some alien's supercomputer. But for the most part we live just like other people do—though with more free time and less fashion sense.

A more plausible interpretation of learning how to die is the one held by the Stoic philosophers. Death is the ulti-

....

[*] The following few paragraphs are adapted from a convocation speech I gave at the University of Toronto in 2014, published as "For Graduates, a Crash Course in Life, Courtesy of Mark Kingwell," *National Post*, November 24, 2014.

mate inconvenient fact, the outcome we cannot alter. We *can* be smart about how to estimate and even be just about the entailed risks of a mortal existence. We can embrace this nothingness, at the limit, and thus defeat the fear of dying. This then opens up the only immortality known to humans, namely, living on in the memory of others.

Which sounds great. But as Woody Allen once said, "I don't want to live on in the hearts of my countrymen. I want to live on in my apartment."

No, I think learning how to die really means living with a sense of urgency and purpose. Only the presence of a deadline can provide this. The added twist is that we don't know, exactly, when the deadline will fall.

Which brings me to risk in a more physical sense. In 1984, I met a man called Raymond Eric "Bill" Loverseed. Loverseed was a colleague of my father's at De Havilland Aircraft, a former member of the Royal Air Force's Red Arrows demonstration team. My father logged more than two thousand air hours as a senior navigator in the Canadian military. As with all course plotters, who just have to sit there while pilots do the flying, he was a keen judge of character. At De Havilland he had survived a couple of close calls with Loverseed at the controls. "An awfully good pilot," my father told me on one occasion. "But he took some wild chances."

Aviators know that every flight entails a risk and every crash is a failure. They also know, however, that there are three kinds of crashes: good crashes, bad crashes, and last crashes.

In 1984, when I met him in London, Loverseed was flying a DHC-5 Buffalo transport plane at the Farnborough Airshow. The highlight was a low pass over the demonstration area, the plane just a couple of metres off the ground. That day, the Hampshire wind backed on him and the plane lost lift suddenly. Loverseed's airspeed was too low to compensate, the plane stalled, and then dropped like a stone. It slammed into the runway and slid to a point a few hundred yards from a crowd of spectators, including me.

That was a good crash: everybody present walked away. I, for one, walked away to get a stiff drink.

Three years later, Loverseed was ferrying a Piper Cherokee from the United States to Britain when he hit a storm off the coast of Newfoundland. The wings of the small plane iced up, and the aircraft plunged almost three thousand metres into dense forest, tearing off both wings as it went. Loverseed's foot was crushed and it was sixteen frigid hours before he was rescued. That was a bad crash.

Then, in 1998, test-flying a De Havilland Dash 7 over Devon after taking off from the Channel Island of Guernsey, he developed engine trouble; the aircraft dipped, and slammed into a hillside near Bickington. Loverseed was killed, as was another colleague of my father's, Adam Saunders of Toronto. That was a last crash.

We can never stop accepting the next flight, the next mission. The last crash makes every hour in the air that much sweeter. And we must all remember the hopeful and sometimes wild command of every pilot as her or his plane sets up at the end of the runway: *Full power now, please.*

* * *

I HAD BEEN writing about risk, specifically in political terms, for some time when the novel coronavirus that produces the disease COVID-19 upended the global order in the pandemic of 2020. Suddenly all thoughts of life risk were reordered. We had all considered, whether idly or urgently, according to circumstance, the chances of death or dismemberment that might attend a given choice or activity. We had, most of us, or those who could afford it, taken out insurance policies of various kinds to stake an odds-based claim on the uncertain future. Few of us, if we were not extremely ill or soldiers or oil-rig workers or North Pacific fishermen, had considered death to be a daily prospect in need of consideration.

And yet of course it was, because it always is. You might get struck by a bus while blithely crossing the street, or gunned down in street crossfire during a drug deal gone wrong, or succumb to pilot error and structural weakness as a jetliner plunges into the sea. The fact that the odds of these mortal occurrences remained low—lower, we were always told, than drowning in your own bathtub or falling to a broken neck off an aluminum utility ladder—might diminish, but could never eliminate, the element of risk that attends each moment of human existence.

The world of the virus made all of this more vivid, and more confused. The slogans that predominated in the early weeks of social distancing and self-isolation—"We're all in this together" and "The virus doesn't discriminate"—were belied by uncomfortable realities. The American death toll alone, about a quarter of the global figure, rose to 80,000 in early May 2020, then past 140,000 in July, with some experts predicting as many as 100,000 new cases every day. This was, as of the Fourth of July, more than the combined fatalities of the Korean, Vietnam, Gulf, Iraq, and Afghanistan wars. At the same time, it was increasingly clear that social and economic fault lines rendered the virus very uneven in distribution. The poor, Black, Latino, aged, and Indigenous sectors of the population were far more vulnerable than other demographic slices. God forbid you should suffer from an intersection of more than one of those descriptors, since that would drive your expected mortality far higher. Risk is never just a matter of mathematical odds; it is also, and always, a matter of who you happen to be demographically. The former is stark but implacable; the latter is frightening but open to potential partial correction.

That demographic factor is itself a matter of dice rolls— what economists and philosophers call the birthright lottery. Who and where and how you find yourself on this mortal plane is a massive, and massively predictable, governor of life outcomes over time. There will always be outliers, to be sure, but there is a reason that statistics, demographics, and actuarial mathematics have reliable purchase on the messy terrain of human life. It is *because they work*: they cannot predict individual outcomes, but they can and do crunch large numbers to deliver valid generalizations. These are not laws, even in the provisional natural-science sense, but they remain implacable and predictive. And therefore, necessarily, inescapable.

Another feature of the global pandemic crisis concerned the nature of planning. I will have more to say about the nature of plans, their aspirations and limits, in a later section of this book; but the most proximate insight about pandemic planning was that there was none. Reacting slowly and after the fact, most governments found themselves in the unenviable position of playing catch-up with a foe that was invisible, ubiquitous, and fickle. The "flatten the curve" strategy adopted by nearly all of these leaders soon began to generate negative economic impacts in the form of job losses, depleted demand, and the systematic ruin of whole sectors, such as entertainment, sports, and restaurants. Retail outlets hung on with curbside pickup and other stopgap measures, but the structural costs of sheltering in place and social distancing were impossible to ignore: downside economic risk coming into play under stark new market conditions. These costs were made worse, in some cases, by the self-serving, boastful, and egomaniacal depredations of President Donald Trump, who single-handedly sowed discord and confusion on a daily basis throughout the spring and summer.*

But even Donald Trump could not shoulder the blame for a general failure of leadership all over the world, from China and India to Brazil and Russia. There is an old military adage that speaks to the issue of necessary redundancy in all planning: "Two is one, and one is none." If you have only one of something, you have nothing. If you only have a single plan, you have no plan at all. Efforts to bolster any Pandemic Plan B, C, D, and other contingencies were met with immediate opposition and even howls of protest, especially if those plans entailed potential mortality rates above the already morbid norms emerging by late spring. And yet these alternate plans might, over a longer term, save lives and

....

* A Facebook post from July 2020: Trump "managed to bring back the 1918 Pandemic, the 1929 Depression, and the 1968 race riots ALL AT THE SAME TIME! Can we all agree that this experiment of having a dumb TV host and shady real estate developer with 6 bankruptcies, 5 kids from 3 different marriages, 11 charges of sexual assault, and 4,000-plus lawsuits as president *is not going well at all*?"

livelihoods; they might allow a bounce-back in the stricken economy. Where once "experts" predicted a V-shaped recovery—sharp plunge followed by sharp rebound—eventually most fell back to U-shaped recovery models, with the most pessimistic noting the chance of W-shaped (false short-term recovery) or even L-shaped curves. (The latter is not a recovery curve at all, just an admission of permanent value loss.)

Two is one, and one is none. At the very moment when risk seemed more proximate than usual, where almost everyone believed that death was potentially imminent—however falsely, given the distributions of privilege and health care access—there was a cognitive gap in the population as blinkered as any youthful belief in immortality. Paraphrasing the harsh wartime wisdom of soldiers, we should be moved to say this: "This will end. Eventually. Before it does, a lot more people have to die." But how many?[*]

This is a book about risk written at an especially risky time. Every trip to the grocery store, every walk around the block, is currently a minefield of contagion chance. The odds here are largely incalculable because, though we can enumerate infections and deaths, we cannot render a good bet on something that travels through the air. But there are no good prophecies now, if there ever were: all the punditry in the world about what post-pandemic life will look like is just so much hot air—and, in contrast to earlier eras of augury, with few attendant risks to the pronouncers

....

[*] Economist Tyler Cowen has predicted a stage of "phantom risk" as the pandemic subsides, meaning alarm attached to non-fatal COVID-19 cases that stalls economic recovery. "[S]ociety will move from seriously underrating pandemic risk to badly overrating it," he predicted. Such phantom risk "will remain a binding constraint even after most of the real dangers are past." Tyler Cowen, "The Phantom Risk of Covid-19," Bloomberg News, August 19, 2020.

even as there might be great costs for economies and societies governed by bad bets. "Ancient augurs and prophets were in high-risk professions," the critic Mark Lilla wrote in the spring of 2020. "Many lost their lives when their predictions failed to materialize, either executed by sovereigns or pulled apart by mobs. We see a bloodless version of this reaction today in the public's declining confidence in both the news media and the government."*

Worse, he notes, are predictions—each no more rational or trustworthy than the next—that only serve to hasten social costs. Thus his own decision, which I will echo here, not to predict or prophesy. This book is inflected (or infected) by the virus, but not precisely about the virus—except as it grants new urgency to old questions of risk and politics. As Lilla wrote: "[T]he post-Covid future doesn't exist. It will exist only after we have made it. Religious prophecy is rational, on the assumption that the future is in the gods' hands, not ours. Believers can be confident that what the gods say through the oracles' mouth or inscribe in offal will come to pass, independent of our actions. But if we don't believe in such deities, we have no reason to ask what will happen to us. We should ask only what we want to happen, and how to make it happen, given the constraints of the moment."

* Mark Lilla, "No One Knows What's Going to Happen," *New York Times*, May 22, 2020. This article naturally did not stop the flood of predictions about post-pandemic life from every pundit from hither and yon, the collective voice of borrowed, superficial pseudo-insight that a friend of mine once named "Gladwell Moore." My favourite of these shadow plays was a panel of head scratchers gathered to make predictions in an article called "Four Futurists on How to Be Forward-Thinking in a Post-COVID-19 World," *Hustle*, May 24, 2020. Their predictions included more 3-D printing and ongoing challenges to sectors such as hospitality and travel. The website aggregator the Morning News labelled their link, laconically, "A panel of futurists, offering tips on how to be forward-thinking right now, proves to be largely as clueless as everybody else."

I started thinking specifically about risk and *community* some months ago, even though the germ of those thoughts was not virus-related but was prompted by an earlier remark by Russian president Vladimir Putin, in 2019, to the effect that "the liberal idea has become obsolete."[*] In common with most political observers, I took this to mean that Putin meant for us to understand that liberal-democratic institutions and the rule of law, at least four centuries in the making but even older in the Roman legal tradition, had been rendered obsolete by populist-authoritarian movements of the early twenty-first century. In my mind, the four hundred–plus years of liberal thought has been about creating community through inclusion of the Other—accommodation of different religions, genders, races, geographies—rather than the exclusion so dominant in other ideas of "community" (based on bloodline, cultural uniformity, shared belief— indeed, most commonly, the shared belief that shared bloodline was even a feature of life).

Putin was correct about then-current "populist" political movements, which were in fact not populist at all but rejections of the liberal idea and hence regressive attacks on the idea of Otherness. The Putin Doctrine, if we can grant such a grandiose title to such a minuscule notion, poses this choice for humanity *circa* 2020: Do you want people to come inside the magic circle of protection and potential affluence, or do you want to keep them out? National borders are the traditional thresholds here, as we were forced to see in Mexico and elsewhere by the

....

* The comment was widely reported. See, for example, Marc Bennetts, "Western Liberalism Is Obsolete, Warns Putin, ahead of May Meeting," *Guardian*, June 28, 2019.

depredations of the American president who demanded that a wall be built and also that someone else pay for it. This is Fortress America, of course, but much magnified.

Here is how writer Ken Kalfus describes the situation in his brilliant novella *Coup de Foudre* (2015), which fictionalizes Dominique Strauss-Kahn's 2011 sexual assault of a Manhattan hotel housekeeper: "Widowed, infected, illiterate, and impoverished, Marianna sought a more humane life for her child in the sanctuary of the West. The sanctuary is heavily guarded; from the outside, it looks more like a fortress, with high-tech, weaponized ramparts. Every day thousands throw themselves at its walls in leaky boats that wash up on the beaches of the Mediterranean, or by trekking through the American desert, or by boarding airplanes with vague dreams and papers that will be contemptuously scrutinized—dreams and papers both."*

It is, or was, also the architectural basis of many parts of Europe. One does not have to see the dead body of a child refugee, washed up on the shores of a Mediterranean coastline, to appreciate the stakes here. The walls are high, and grow higher by the day.

But that was then, and this is now. The pandemic is no respecter of national borders—though its effects were felt disproportionately, as always, according to race and class. What, then, of community, and the very idea of inclusion? Before, the main problem was walls: some figurative (financial, cultural), some material (border fences, passport checkpoints). Now the problem of community

---

* Ken Kalfus, *Coup de Foudre: A Novella and Stories* (New York: Bloomsbury, 2015), 52. Kalfus's story originally appeared in *Harper's Magazine* (April 2014).

becomes one where walls and borders, indeed thresholds of all previous kinds, simply do not apply.

* * *

LET US, THEN, foreground the idea of community under these conditions—which are not so much *new* as more *vivid*, which is to say, more willing to limn the contours of reality. This will be both a starting point and an end-game for the present short book.

One's thoughts and memories turn, maybe unwillingly, to Thomas Robert Malthus's "principle of population."[*] There is geometric increase in population, Malthus contentiously argued, but only linear increase in food. Hence there would be an inevitable eventual famine, or a resource scarcity of some other disastrous kind. Malthus considered this a natural condition of limited ecospheres with rigid boundaries. Thus the need, he argued, for either drastic redistribution of resources, or else constantly renewed and expanded growth to relieve the pressure.

But there are going to be limits on the latter, and political objections to the former. Malthus ignores the possibility of expanding the limits of ecospheres, and makes his geometric-arithmetical logic unassailable. Those are clear conceptual errors. But he is perhaps correct that there are boundaries beyond which we cannot adapt, and he also implies by example that the politics of panic will be focused on control rather than co-operation.

Any situation of hard resource limit is bad enough,

....

[*] See T.R. Malthus, *An Essay on the Principle of Population* [orig. 1798, expanded version 1803, Appendix 1806], ed. Joyce E. Chaplin (New York: W.W. Norton, 2017).

and arguably was part of the pre-pandemic reality even when correcting for the lack of nuance in Malthus. Now suppose that you expand "food" to mean resources more generally, or indeed the entire biosphere. The issues return with renewed force. Malthus thought there would be demographic "corrections" when overcrowding and demand created crisis: famines, obviously, but also pestilence and disease; and, of course, war—now understood clearly as a conflict over control of land and associated resources. Ideology is in play here, as are motivating notions of honour and courage in battle, but mostly as window dressing for basic depredation and conquest of desirable property. It is impossible to ignore the economics of war, whether virtual, viral, or material.

Thus we arrive very quickly indeed at our current moment, where "herd immunity" is another way of saying "vulnerable-demographic firebreak" on the spread of virus under conditions of resource limits. This is the only viable alternative to a safe, early, and universally available vaccine, which remains the gold standard for overcoming any pandemic. The goal, said public health expert David Katz, "is natural herd immunity, achieved by those of us at low risk for severe infection, who can most safely go back to work and school and life as we knew it, while taking the right, reasonable protections. Meanwhile, we should guard those most vulnerable until we can sound the all-clear. Only this kind of thoughtful, risk-stratified approach can allow for herd immunity with maximal safety and minimal total harm from infection and the consequences of prolonged lockdown alike."[*]

* Quoted in Thomas L. Friedman, "Is Trump Trying to Spread Covid-19?" *New York Times*, June 16, 2020. "It is absolutely devilish," Friedman wrote, "like

With viruses such as this one, however, as much as 70 percent of the population might need to contract it in order to protect the overall herd. Suppose this can actually be done. The semi-palatable versions of the risk stratification and herd immunity strategies typically then break into *natural* and *forced* options. The natural option is the scenario in which enough of a given population shows immunity to a virus to halt further spread. The forced option might include *variolation* (as with smallpox, where infected tissue becomes the basis of a vaccine) or volunteer infection, which singles out segments of the population for controlled infection and the resulting collection of antibodies. There is a third option, namely vaccination, to introduce overall immunity directly—albeit very slowly.

The brutal version of the thesis, by contrast, is this: we should simply open up the population to viral spread, especially if the effects of other, less radical measures include irreparable economic damage. Let the old, sick, and poor bear the brunt of the virus-based population "correction" so that the young, healthy, and wealthy can continue the human race.

If we attempt to limit the virus's spread with mitigating measures that distribute the risks across the entire population, the overall death tolls may be lower, but the cumulative costs of all kinds will be much higher. The firebreak metaphor is apt: we should allow deadwood to burn, or even burn some of it ourselves, in order to keep the forest fire from engulfing the entire hillside. Trying to

----

Trump wakes up every morning and asks himself: What health expert's advice can I defy today? What simple gesture to reduce the odds that the coronavirus continues to surge, post-lockdowns, can I ignore today? What quack remedy can I promote today?"

reduce the fire's force by dousing it at the advance edge saves marginally more trees overall but causes other kinds of far-reaching damage to the environment.

We are talking about people and not trees. The conversation about viral countermeasures and the timeline for "liberating" the economy is muddy because we are not simply brutal, even as we also feel long-term pressures that are scary. One idea of ethical response (flatten the curve, ride out the viral storm, keep economic curbs in place for a long time even if that is very costly) competes with another ethical theory—almost too nasty to speak about—whereby "selective" reopening of the economy is exchanged for a "reasonable" death toll.

We can solve the food problem if we manage, through innovation and better distribution—not to mention curbs on insane waste rates in the so-called developed world— to match population growth with resource growth. There are untapped resources of sustainable nourishment in our oceans and fields. (Hint: beef is probably not on the long-term future menu.)

But we know that many resources are non-renewable and non-expandable by definition, not just through mismanagement and poor distribution. These are goods that are, in economic parlance, private if not in fact positional: competitive, double-rival, and double-excludable resources where your use entails my suffering. This situation, in fact, represents the very pinnacle of private goods versus public ones.

The category of private-perhaps-positional goods right now includes health care, which has become a series of zero-sum games even under a public health system: my respirator is a respirator you can't have; so is my hospital bed, and the attention of my nurse or physician. We keep trying to parse health as a public good when the truth is that, at point of distribution, it is anything but.

Social fault lines are exposed by the virus, and can only yawn wider. This is so within societies: rich versus poor on access to care, but also on access to online education, for example, or the ability to stay home and still pay the bills, bake our sourdough bread, and watch Netflix. It is a bad time to be Black in America and Indigenous in Canada (when was it not?), and to be poor anywhere. But there are also emergent competitions between nations and regions. Governors of American states competing for respirators and testing reagents are small change compared with the affliction of the virus on areas already suffering hunger, lack of clean water and reliable access to medication, and so on. We have, and had, no idea how all the global inequality is going to be exacerbated by the pandemic. As I write, some public health experts are puzzled that there are not more cases in Africa, though this may simply be a function of limited testing. As the American president doesn't seem to understand, tests do not create cases, they reveal them. Kind of a big difference.

Meanwhile, we in the so-called "developed" world have been living in a resource-rich fantasyland of apparent prosperity and taken-for-granted comfort. It is and always has been a house of cards. Consider Malthus once again: environmental crisis is unpredictable, and so are its results. Even the thickest cocoons can be breached, and not all the dead are the poor. The contrastive claim is likewise true: not all the suffering will be borne by the reckless and the feckless, the young-and-restless, brainless "covidiots" clustered on newly opened Florida beaches, in Texas and Arizona bars, or gathering for rallies at the dangerously incompetent president's urging—to celebrate him, and to protest "tyrannical" public health measures in Minnesota, Virginia, and Michigan (early 2020) and then Georgia, Texas, and Arkansas (mid-2020). It would be hard for alien observers to understand that actual gunfights have broken out over the idea that someone should take an obvious precaution such as wearing a mask.

Well, maybe not—if those same aliens have been watching us long enough. Humans are clever when it comes to their own self-preservation, but they can also be monumentally stupid. Perhaps unfortunately, Darwin's principle of natural selection only targets the dumb when measured over large numbers and spans of time. In the short term, wealthy dummies have a better chance of survival than even the most intelligent members of vulnerable subpopulations.

* * *

ONE FEATURE OF pandemic thinking worth singling out in terms of risk is the peddling of conspiracy theories, or more basically the rotten ideology of *conspiracism*, a toxic variant of what historian Richard Hofstadter called "the paranoid style in American politics."* Conspiracism isn't this or that particular conspiracy theory—the COVID-19 virus is a media hoax, a Chinese false flag operation, an effort by Bill

....

* Originally Hofstadter's Herbert Spencer Lecture at Oxford University (21 November 1963), then first published in *Harper's Magazine* (November 1964), finally expanded in *The Paranoid Style in American Politics, and Other Essays* (New York: Vintage, 1964).

Gates to generate new profits, a function of 5G cellphone towers—but the very idea that there is something, someone, somewhere who is in charge of what is going on.[*] When the sitting president of the United States, still unironically referred to as "the greatest nation on Earth," which is to say *right now* the one with the highest per capita pandemic death rate, encourages and abets these insane efforts, the effects go from laughable to actively dangerous. These are not just fringe wackadoodles anymore, when they have sanction and support from the demented, paranoid, ego-shadowing White House of 2020.[†]

As debunkers of conspiracy have long pointed out, we are simply *not that smart or well-organized*—no, not even Beijing or Bill Gates. Things happen, often for no central or logical reason, even if your logic is already badly twisted and deranged. Conspiracy is a form of naive theism: a belief that there is a controlling intelligence, albeit a cruel or deceitful one, and that this fact therefore makes sense of an apparently senseless world! There is in fact no solace here, any more than there is from more traditional and legitimate forms of theism. God will not save us or explain

....

[*] Frederick Kaufman, "Pandemics Go Hand in Hand with Conspiracy Theories," *New Yorker*, May 13, 2020. "Distrust accrues in quarantine, perhaps for good reason: our most intimate home—our metabolism—has turned into a potential subversive. Our own bodies can betray us, unknowingly becoming the sources of contagion." For a deft satirical takedown of Internet-spawned delusions, see Tabatha Southey, "Coronaviruses, conspiracies and the rise of broadbanditry," *Maclean's*, May 8, 2020. Choice quotation, on the theory that Bill Gates engineered the deadly coronavirus in order to deploy a vaccine as a data-gathering device: "Now take a moment to enjoy the irony that people who are convinced that a tech billionaire might be collecting all of their personal information and monitoring their contacts for nefarious reasons are complaining about it on Facebook."

[†] See, for example, evidence of Donald Trump's support for the conspiracy group QAnon, as reported by Mike McIntire and Kevin Roose, "What Happens When QAnon Seeps from the Web to the Offline World," *New York Times*, February 9, 2020. But of course we know that this is just fake news!

our condition; neither will central intelligence, space aliens, hidden forces, or global cabals. Mostly, stupidity is a more valid general explanation for bad things happening than centralized malice.* In current conditions, a virus is a natural condition much closer to a zombie than to a god: pointless, without purpose except death, relentless, and rapidly viral. Indeed, zombies are the all-purpose metaphor for such contagion—even as they have been analyzed, in theory, as a kind of pandemic themselves.†

The basic question of all human societies has been: Who will live and who will die? This is what the philosopher Achille Mbembé expressed in a 2003 essay called "Necropolitics": "The ultimate expression of sovereignty resides, to a large degree, in the power and capacity to dictate who may live and who must die. Hence, to kill or allow to live constitutes the limits of sovereignty, its fundamental attributes."‡ *That* is what

....

* This is a version of what has come, through somewhat shadowy provenance, to be known as Hanlon's Razor, often attributed to a Pennsylvania man who supplied a version of it to a Murphy's Law joke book. It has sometimes been compared to Occam's Razor, named for philosopher William of Ockham (1285–1347), which advises "do not multiply entities needlessly," or as often (but not quite accurately) paraphrased: the simplest explanation of a phenomenon is to be preferred over any more complex one.

† Canadian researchers, modelling rates of infection and difficulty of eradication, determined in 2009 that an actual zombie attack would indeed destroy human societies in a very short time unless public health countermeasures were swift and decisive.

  Significantly, they generated their models based on the traditional slow zombie, which is presumably easier to kill; an attack of *28 Days Later*–style fast zombies would likely be too virulent to counter. See P. Munz, I. Hudea, J. Imad, and R.J. Smith? [the punctuation is part of his proper name], "When Zombies Attack! Mathematical Modelling of an Outbreak of Zombie Infection," in *Infectious Diseases Modelling Research Progress*, ed. Jean Michel Tchuenche and C. Chiyaka (New York: Nova Publishers, 2011), 133–50. (Small, uncanny foot-footnote: Nova Publishers has been flagged as a vanity or predatory press—an academic zombie, in fact.)

‡ J.-A. Mbembé, "Necropolitics," trans. Libby Meintjes, *Public Culture* 15:1 (Winter 2003): 11–40.

sovereignty means, friends. Which is why risk management is really about death management—even though
we don't like to say so. The existential baseline beneath
those calculations is John Maynard Keynes's famous
socio-economic conclusion: "In the long run, we are all
dead." True enough (and, for Keynes, more about mon-
etary policy than life philosophy); but, in the present,
we need to be thinking hard about when, why, and how
many are dead, not just lurching from reaction to reaction. The virus is neither brutal nor just; it simply is.
This is an unplanned challenge, a force of nature. What
it portends and achieves is up to us.

The story of risk is a narrative: of despair or hope, of
doom or rescue, of wins and losses. The mortal limits are
drawn by the physical world, as always. The narrative limits
are drawn, indeed really *created*, by us. That story is about
who we are and what we value within the frame of enforced
individual and, maybe, collective death. At the end of this
book I will return to an idea of collective death—species
apocalypse—and try to think through what that could
mean for those who go before such an endgame.

Perhaps we can forestall apocalypse, but not by any
simple return to the past. Justice in a risky world does not
mean a return to normal, whatever normal might seem
to mean. It starts, at least, with a recognition that the
normal was deeply and inherently unjust. There were
already population firebreaks before the pandemic, brutal
mechanisms of immunity constructed of barbed wire
fencing and birthright exclusion. New firebreaks of the
reckless and stupid are not defensible in current dis-
courses about disease and risk, which is a victory for
decency but maybe a defeat for global equity.

Meanwhile, we lurch on into our near future, caught between the dilemmatic horns of mass death and economic collapse. Is there any resolution here? We must hope so, but whatever it is will not, and should not, mean a return to what went before. The risks there are only too obvious, including what some, prominently economist Robin Hanson, have called the collective delusion of *dream time*. This term identifies the seemingly natural but in fact aberrant period during which cheap energy and credit, low birth rates, and unrivalled sense of entitlement have erected an impregnable fortress of comfort for those living inside, excluding the masses without.[*]

That fortress is not just material. It is also ideological, discursive, and at least purportedly rational. But disease is like risk more generally: it is in one basic sense entirely uninterested in human desire, ambition, and pretension. It has no ideology, religion, or inherent cultural biases. "The only thing it wants is targets," George Mason University computer scientist Adam Elkus wrote of the coronavirus in March 2020.[†]

"It does not think," Elkus continued, "it does not feel, and it lies totally outside the elaborate social nuances humans have carved out through patterns of communication, representation and discourse. And this, above all else, makes it a lethal adversary for the West. It has exposed how much of Western society … is permeated with influential people who have deluded themselves into thinking that their ability to manipulate words, images

[*] One of Hanson's earliest posts on the topic was "This Is the Dream Time," *Overcoming Bias*, September 28, 2009. His book *The Age of Em: Work, Love, and Life When Robots Rule the Earth* (New York: Oxford University Press, 2018) is also valuable.

[†] Adam Elkus, "It Only Wants Targets," *Glitch* blog post (March 13, 2020).

and sounds gives them the ability to control reality itself."

And then this: "There were endless attempts early on to compare it to a less-threatening entity, the flu or even the common cold. In doing so, institutional actors tried to take something new and uncertain and fit it into a tame pre-existing mental model that they preferred. Acknowledging the virus as a creature of fate—of *fortuna*—would be to admit that it could collapse the elaborate machinery for making narrative and reveal the narrative-makers as utterly impotent." But the narrative, and its political makers, have proven very resilient. It is our job, as citizens, to fashion a better story, a liberatory one, where this crisis is in fact an opportunity. In the pages that follow, I am going to delve a little more deeply into the politics and philosophy of risk, but always with an eye to a more equitable future as we emerge, haltingly, from our current status.

So now, trying as best we can while still living through it, and acknowledging all that has occurred since the first days of the 2020 pandemic, we must move on to the next staging ground of contingency, through narrow passes of possibility, thin defiles with potential threat on both sides of the march. Advance cautiously and watch for flanking fire or strafing runs—otherwise known as emergent unforeseen risks, the kinds that cut down from the sides or the air. There will be bad weather, bad luck, disease, disaster, and death. But we have no choice but to continue the frontal assault of the present into the future.

Houses of both cards and brick will surely collapse before this latest challenge to human complacency and decadence has finished its deadly work. Privilege may or may not be challenged; already in the spring of 2020 it was obvious that the effects of viral infection were being disproportionately suffered by those of low income and non-white race. Financial markets and those who benefit from them were recovering. Countries with the means and might to do so were closing their borders more tightly than ever, even as they attempted to corner markets on personal protective equipment and future potential vaccines. The rights of nations once more seemed to shove aside any notion of universal human rights.

And yet there were, at the same time, many signs of hope—not of optimism in the superficial sense, but of the apparently senseless and yet basic need for humans to believe that there will always be another chance. Risk and hope go together, sometimes for ill but often enough for good, to make the demonstrably uncaring universe seem, now and then, at least minimally hospitable. What more can we humans ask, or expect?

By the summer of 2020, the "Black Lives Matter" and "I Can't Breathe" protests over the killing of George Floyd by Minneapolis policemen had succeeded, perhaps unwittingly, in dismantling the logic of curve-flattening, physical distancing, and lockdown. If these large gatherings, which necessarily included shouting protesters and close body contact, were permissible, why wasn't a sports event or concert? One can draw distinctions on risk, but they should, critics insisted, at least be consistent distinctions. These protests are, in my own view, worth the risk—but is that just special pleading in favour of a cause I believe in?*

....

* The point was made, *contra* prevailing spirits, by Ross Douthat, including references to Adam Elkus's post cited earlier, in "Why the Coronavirus Is Winning," *New York Times*, June 6, 2020.

It is worth noting that, sadly but unsurprisingly, the issue of the protests, like mask wearing and other observances, quickly became fodder for the divisive culture wars that lately afflict the United States and, to a lesser extent, Canada. For every triumphant conservative mocking the protesters for abandoning distancing rules, there was a public health expert touting an unexpected utilitarian logic whereby anti-racism protests save more lives than the ones put at risk by proximity during public rallies.[*]

One American journalist wrote eloquently about the suspicion and hostility she observed when wearing a mask in the American South.[†] Such conflicts were not just to be observed in the United States. I was myself called out in vile terms—the epithet "virtue-signalling asshole" was used—for wearing a mask in my own Cabbagetown neighbourhood of Toronto. Another twitchy fellow citizen, crowding me in the pharmacy pickup line, wanted to engage in philosophy debate. This encounter occurred on the first day of mandated mask-wearing in shared indoor spaces. I said, "You should be wearing a mask." He responded by launching into a peculiar monologue about the difference between "should" and "ought" that reminded me powerfully of some of my more boring philosophy colleagues, but which fell well short of gunplay. And, to be fair, the main drag here in my part of the city, Parliament Street, has always been an uneasy mix of

....

[*] Compare Rex Murphy, "Is Physical Distancing Over? It Sure Seems to Be," *National Post*, June 8, 2020; and Brian Resnick, "What Public Health Experts Want Critics to Know about Why They Support the Protests," *Vox*, June 6, 2020. This second piece is noteworthy for coining a new phrase: "second-wave systemic racism," which is argued to be far more deadly than any second wave of the coronavirus.

[†] Margaret Renki, "What It's Like to Wear a Mask in the South," *New York Times*, June 1, 2020.

oddballs, meth-heads, long-time merchant families, and gentrifying white-liberal jerks like me.

Even as these mini-conflicts were being played out, it was made clear over and over that at least two issues of risk affect Black people, and other North American racial minorities, more than the complacent white majority who make up the bulk of mask refusers and other anti-science militants.

The first is that pandemic fallout has fallen disproportionately on Black Americans, Indigenous people, migrant farm workers, and others who live in crowded neighbourhoods where service industries dominate the employment picture. In some districts, such as Chicago, the 30 percent Black population has witnessed 70 percent of COVID-related deaths. In Wisconsin, with a Black population of just 6 percent, the number of Black viral deaths is half the state total. None of this should be surprising. The obvious factors in the statistical warp include front-line jobs, the necessity of using public transportation, lack of health care coverage, pre-existing conditions such as diabetes, and crowded living conditions. All of these are structural-justice issues that make it such that a virus, while theoretically and epidemiologically neutral and random, is not actually above politics.[*] In Canada, we find similar statistics with respect to Indigenous people, usually for similar reasons, including pre-existing health conditions and widespread lack of access to clean water.[†]

....

[*] See, for example, Emma Greg Ellis, "Covid-19 Is Killing Black People Unequally—Don't Be Surprised," *Wired*, May 2, 2020.

[†] Amanda Carling and Insiya Mankani, "Systemic Inequities Increase Covid-19 Risk for Indigenous People in Canada," *Human Rights Watch*, June 9, 2020.

The second major risk factor for non-whites predates current conditions, namely the fact that being Black—or, in Canada, Indigenous—statistically raises any individual's chances of experiencing a violent encounter with police, incarceration, and even death at the hands of the state. To consider just rates of incarceration, which are easiest to track, fully one-third of Canada's imprisoned population is Indigenous, despite their making up just 5 percent of the national population.[*] The numbers from the United States indicate that a Black person is five times more likely than a white to end up behind bars—an improved rate measured against the six-times-greater likelihood that prevailed for decades before the turn of the millennium.[†]

It therefore follows, by proven population rules, that it is *inherently and inescapably more risky* to be a Black or Indigenous person, all things considered. In the United States it is especially dangerous to be a young Black man, and in Canada to be a young Indigenous woman. These last distinctions count simply as finer degrees of awfulness within the larger heinous pattern of unequal risk distribution.

* * *

THUS, SOME MORE philosophically inclined pundits tried to situate the larger conflicts not in utilitarian logics but in a well-known but often misunderstood distinction, drawn from Isaiah Berlin, between *negative* and *positive*

---

[*] Leyland Cecco, "'National Travesty': Report Shows One Third of Canada's Prisoners Are Indigenous," *Guardian*, January 22, 2020.

[†] Katie Mettler, "States Imprison Black People at Five Times the Rate of Whites—a Sign of a Narrowing yet Still-Wide Gap," *Washington Post*, December 4, 2019.

liberty.* Crudely, negative liberty is freedom *from*: from constraint, from censorious limit, from government interference. Positive liberty is freedom *to*: to belong, to maximize a vision of justice, to be part of something larger than myself. American politics, especially at the libertarian fringes, finds the former sacrosanct and the latter intolerable.

As *New Yorker* writer Masha Gessen noted in May 2020, "Late last week, a video compilation started making the rounds, showing customers in public places of business—Costco, Walmart, a Red Lobster—refusing to wear masks or to observe social distancing, and, when called out on their negligence, demonstratively coughing and even spitting on the mostly low-wage employees who were trying to enforce basic safety guidelines." And so: "These are the images of the current culture war, fought and framed, like other American culture wars, around conflicting ideas of freedom. 'I woke up in a free country,' a disgruntled Costco customer says. 'What freedom is being sacrificed by wearing a mask?' a Twitter user asks. 'The freedom to not wear a fucking mask,' another responds."†

Gessen attempted to navigate this reef of shoals but only ended up emphasizing the basic problem: "For a sense of common cause to appear, there has to be a sense of *us*: a community that is facing a threat and mounting a response. But we have vastly different experiences of the pandemic and vastly different expectations of the government. The

....

* Isaiah Berlin, *Two Concepts of Liberty* (Oxford: Clarendon Press, 1958). Berlin originally delivered this essay as his inaugural Oxford professorial lecture on October 31, 1958; it was later reprinted in his *Four Essays on Liberty* (Oxford: Oxford University Press, 1969).

† Masha Gessen, "Life, Liberty, and the Pursuit of Spitting on Other People," *New Yorker*, May 26, 2020.

anti-mask people in the viral videos are all white, and, it appears, all or most of them live in suburbs or exurbs. They seem to see mask-wearing as a kind of tyrannical virtue-signalling; they expect to be served and assume they are safe, both from the virus and from facing any consequences for flouting the rules or physically harming others."

Exactly. And, worse, the fragmentation of shared community has been in large measure fomented, even created, by political factions. Media sources have become hyper-partisan, embubbled, and more openly hysterical. They are echo chambers, but also force multipliers, of their viewers' attitudes and prejudices. With the example of President Trump at the fore, denial and outright falsehood stand alongside insincere performative apologies and cynical or craven assertions of righteousness.[*]

It is then reasonable to ask whether Berlin's famous distinction even holds conceptually. Can you separate freedom to go about your business (negative, one imagines) from the freedom to spend money and enjoy commercial opportunities (positive, surely, since it depends on markets, currency, and infrastructure)? Nevertheless, philosophical niceties aside, there were clear physical risk-conflicts observable in, for example, those who chose to spit on people demanding they wear a mask in order to enter a given store, or carrying guns to rallies opposing any sort of government control on commerce or public gathering.

Danger simply goes on; that's just what it does, what it always has done. It is at base indiscriminate, inescapable, and incendiary. But its effects are not equitable by a long

....

[*] Mark Kingwell, "The Science of Denial," *Maclean's*, July 13, 2020.

throw. Only human choice, action, and policy make a *danger* into a *risk*, a conceptual distinction we will see illuminated in the following pages. And with human choice, action, and policy we are in the realm of the political, because everything is indeed political—including the apparently apolitical threats of viral contagion and painful, lingering death.

Nothing can be *solved* right here and right now. Even epidemiological experts are drastically divided over both public health measures and private choices about how to negotiate insurmountable hazards. The *New York Times*, never a slouch in basic reporting, surveyed over *five hundred* of them to prove this obvious point "about what risks are worth taking in the age of coronavirus."* The graphic illustration accompanying this exhaustive, and frankly exhausting, tally—yes I will fly to London, no I will not fly to Hong Kong—was all you really needed to know: "Well, It Depends," the image said.

It *always* depends. It's *always* complicated. The best we can do, even while noting the limits of our discursive power over reality, is thoughtfully examine and reflect on our assumptions and ideas about risk. That is what this short work aims to do. It is no more than a beginning, never an end, nor the beginning of the end. It may just be part, to paraphrase Winston Churchill, who was no Donald Trump when it came to risk, of the end of the beginning.

We fight on, because we have to—and, better yet, also because it is right.

....

* Quoctrung Bui, Claire Cain Miller, and Margot Sanger-Katz, "When 511 Epidemiological Experts Expect to Fly, Hug and Do 18 Other Everyday Activities Again," *New York Times*, June 8, 2020.

1. The Game of Risk

THOSE OF US of a certain age and demographic, which is to say middle-class, mostly white males born in the 1960s and maybe early 1970s, remember a board game called Risk. The original game had been invented in 1957 by a French filmmaker called Albert Lamorisse, who may have inspired the Situationist philosopher Guy Debord, famous for his book *The Society of the Spectacle* (1967). In 1987 Debord created his own military strategy board game, A Game of War.* As with A Game of War, the earlier Risk featured elements of territory, movement, time, and power in a simulation not just of war itself but also—as with more abstract games such as chess and Go—the very ideas of strategy and tactics.

In his autobiography, Debord said the following about his board game creation: "So I have studied the logic of

....

* Once thought lost to circumstance, the game is now available in replica form. Given that I am both a philosophy nerd and a gaming enthusiast, it will come as no surprise that I have a copy of Debord's contribution to board game history, which I demonstrate in graduate seminars on Situationism.

war. Indeed I succeeded long ago in representing its essential movements on a rather simple game-board." He went on: "I played this game, and in the often difficult conduct of my life drew a few lessons from it—setting rules for my life, and abiding by them. The surprises vouchsafed by this *Kriegspiel* of mine seem endless." Among those lessons was a personal one: "I rather fear it may turn out to be the only one of my works to which people will venture to accord any value."*

The larger argument that modelled conflict can induce life lessons is on point. We play these games to learn about vulnerability and danger, not to prepare ourselves for military careers. It's true that the days-long games of Risk I played during the early 1970s were shared with boys who lived on the same military base as I did, but none of us, so far as I was aware, thought we were engaged in training for future induction in the armed forces. In fact, with very few exceptions, my friends from that time had nothing to do with the military after they left high school.

The world of Risk is at once simple to see and devilishly complex to conquer, easily viewed and yet full of hidden surprises. The board itself depicted a global map divided into forty-two territories on six continents. A minimum of two and maximum of six players control armies that attempt to secure these territories, with the

----

* Guy Debord, *Panegyric*, trans. James Brook and John McHale (London: Verso, 1989). One ingenious feature of Debord's game is that, while movement of troops and *matériel* is slow because they are governed by logistics and terrain, transmission of intelligence is virtually instant—if sometimes garbled. This would seem at once to mesh with and to comment upon Paul Virilio's contentions in *Speed and Politics: An Essay on Dromology* (orig. *Vitesse et Politique*, Paris: Galilée, 1977; English translation, New York: Semiotext(e), 1986), namely, (a) that military need drives technological advances, including speed, and (b) that the logical end point of all speed is instantaneity, when the ratio of distance over time is zero.

ultimate (and obvious) goal of total global domination: the original French title of the game was La Conquête du Monde. Parker Brothers, the American publishers, first called it Risk: The Continental Game and then later, maybe because that was considered too vague or French, Risk: The Game of Global Domination. In the game, alliances are encouraged, but so is the sudden dissolution of them for strategic advantage. Guile and subterfuge, even outright deception, are rewarded. Players have a "secret mission" option that can shorten the game by way of coups of various kinds. The action is governed by the appropriately revealing arbitrariness of dice rolls.

Nevertheless, the game was instructively endless, at least in my experience. Having more than two players increased the fun, as well as the social aspect of all gaming; but it also meant, in a fashion I would later see foreshadowed in George Orwell's *Nineteen Eighty-Four*, a perpetual series of self-replicating power struggles among alliances, the way Oceania, Eurasia, and Eastasia maintain years of authoritarian rule under the umbrella of temporary co-operation and permanent conflict. My friends and I were victims of the triumph of hope over experience. We would begin each game with a sense of optimistic, even bloodthirsty, martial ambition. Soon, though, the power struggles would bog down in negotiations, attacks, and counterattacks, and a seemingly interminable flow of power back, forth, and across the cartographic globe.

It seems all too clear to me now that Risk was a strange cultural symptom of the Cold War paranoia that gripped the world in the 1950s and '60s. Depending on your definitions of *cold* and *war*, that spectral conflict, a background

condition created by emergent Eastern and Western blocs
after the defeat of Nazi Germany in 1945, started in 1947
with the Truman Doctrine of Soviet containment and did
not end until the 1991 dissolution of the Soviet Union. By
that reckoning, my entire life from before birth until I finished my last graduate degree and finally got a decent job
was enacted under its chilly conditions.

My friends and I weren't interested in actual global
politics; we just wanted to pass the time, in an era before
video games or the Internet, before cable television or
multiplex cinemas. We had to make our own fun. This
mostly involved quasi-feral outings in the open fields of
Prince Edward Island and Manitoba, where we ran and
biked like loosened demons, with packed lunches of
PB&Js and Thermos Kool-Aid in our knapsacks, over grass
and sand. Injuries were common, from a scraped knee
every other day or so to serious things like a deep gash
from a chain-link fence we were sneaking through, a dog
bite to the face, a cut finger from somebody's radio-con-
trolled model airplane, and a spectacularly bloody nicked
eyelid from the lever of an incorrectly loaded air rifle.
And that was just me, all in one year.

Whenever I incurred similar injuries later in life—a
dislocated shoulder and bone-deep shin laceration while
fly-fishing, a broken leg and half-body abrasions from colliding my ten-speed with a car—I thought back to these
risky young days when our mothers let us run free. We
were not cocooned or swathed. The only helicopters we
encountered were not overprotective parents but the little mechanical gas-nitro ones we actually flew. Risk was
life, indeed *life* was just life. To be honest, we didn't even
really think about risk, being instead unwitting subjects

in the experiment of *not* cocooning a fragile vessel against all jolts and jostles. "Just be home before dark," my mother would say as I headed out for the day, rain or shine, summer or winter. When I was very young, she still set me loose in the neighbourhood without supervision, but with a note pinned to my snowsuit or Hang Ten T-shirt, noting my name and address. Return child to sender—or non-sender, really, maybe even neglecter.

I know I'm idealizing this 1960s-era degree of childhood freedom, and an air force base is already by design an enclosed space, a kind of gated community—without the high-end housing or backyard swimming pools. This was all before the world got more savvy to predatory serial killers and child abductors. It was also before I knew about the infamous Steven Truscott case in which, on an air force base in Ontario where we would later live, a kid not that much older than I was accused and convicted of the rape and murder of a young girl.* (In 2007, Truscott's conviction was overturned for lack of reliable forensic evidence.) But I can't help thinking that these early risks acted, somewhat paradoxically, as inoculations against more deadly diseases and disasters. This is a view with both psychological and popular support.†

....

* The incident is fictionalized brilliantly in Ann-Marie MacDonald's novel *The Way the Crow Flies* (Toronto: Knopf Canada, 2003). MacDonald, an air force brat like me, gets the details of base life exactly right, including the standard country-wide design of the houses, known as PMQS (permanent married quarters). Since most of us moved every two or three years, they were permanent only in the sense of not being tents or Quonset huts.

† For example, Miranda Featherstone, "Resist Fear-Based Parenting," *New York Times*, June 26, 2020. Matthew Crawford, author of *Shop Class as Soulcraft* (New York: Penguin, 2009), has also lately emerged as a proponent of early risk-taking in children. I am prepared to believe that this is more sound than the slightly demented shouts of my military Scoutmaster, who told us that nearly freezing to death during winter camping and orienteering sorties in Manitoba "builds character." For the record, I loved shop class, where I got

When I meet people, especially my university-age students, racked by fear about *unsafe environments* or *microaggressions*, I am torn about how to respond. I want to honour their feelings, even while I am forced to wonder whether they really understand the nature of safety and aggression. An environment in which someone— even someone in power—disagrees with you is not, by that fact, made unsafe; a passive-aggressive verbal slight is decidedly a harm, albeit one most of us can shrug off or complain about later, but it is not the same as a lynching, a house-burning, or a death by police chokehold. Let us please be scalar, if not heedless. University is, whatever else it is, a privileged environment set off from the actually mortal risks of making your way in the world.* Risk is always, and always must be, about perspective— and we humans are not so great at recognizing that, or calculating its effects.

Other parts of the self-made fun that marked my childhood and adolescence were generated indoors rather than in the semi-wild of the Cabot Cove beaches or the flat prairie fields beyond Winnipeg's Perimeter Highway. This included fashioning elaborate plastic scale models of cars and airplanes, long sessions of Dungeons & Dragons, equally long rounds of table hockey, and— maybe best of all—trying to crush our enemies by securing territory by force of arms, lying to and sometimes betraying allies, and resorting to whatever dirty

....

to fool around with power tools and disassembled cars.

* This is one of the few points on which I agree with the world view of my polemical and lately somewhat deranged University of Toronto colleague, Jordan Peterson, who made this very point during a panel discussion on student mental health on which we both appeared (Victoria College, University of Toronto, 2014).

tricks we could imagine. Apart from cartoons on television, when we were allowed to watch them in closely
monitored sessions, the board game Risk was for some
months and years our young world, our miniature global
life.* And so, without knowing it, my friends and I were
being shaped into budding disciples of modern *realpolitik*
in the mode of Napoleon Bonaparte.

On October 2, 1808, the great French field marshal
convened with the German literary genius Johann Wolf-
gang von Goethe in the town of Erfurt. After criticizing
Goethe's literary work with practically Trumpian arrogance—it was too fanciful, Napoleon asserted—Goethe
reported that "He went on to talk about destiny plays,
criticizing them. They belonged to the dark ages. 'Why
these days do they keep giving us destiny?' he said.
'There's no destiny, only politics.'" A more famous version
of the claim is expressed this way: there is no fate but
politics. Fate—the assumption that human outcomes are
determined by the gods, inescapable and cruel, rather
than by human will as it meets the contingencies of the
world—is a thing of the past: ancient, not modern.

....

* Given the recent millennial-generation resurgence of board games, and even
cafés and bars devoted to their play—at least until the non-essential-service
crackdowns of 2020—it is perhaps predictable that there are, since the advent
of the new millennium, versions of Risk that reference J.R.R. Tolkien's *The Lord
of the Rings*, the *Star Wars* universe, C.S. Lewis's Narnia novels, the Transform-
ers franchise, *Doctor Who*, George R.R. Martin's *Game of Thrones* world, *Star
Trek*, and the video games *Call of Duty* and *Assassin's Creed*—among others.

Worth noting, too, is the cooperative board game called Pandemic, first
developed in 2004, after the sars virus. According to cultural observer
Neima Jahromi, the game "was a staple of the short-lived gift shop at the
Centers for Disease Control and Prevention—eventually jostling for shelf
space among Hasbro stalwarts like Monopoly and Clue in Walmarts across
the country. A favorite among doctors battling the coronavirus, Pandemic
has grown from curiosity to cathartic release, offering, in miniature, a finite
version of our stricken world." See Neima Jahromi, "The Board-Game Series
for the Age of the Coronavirus," *New Yorker*, July 27, 2020.

Risk's instructions noted that contests might last hours or days. So we would pause play now and then, to go outside or eat lunch or watch television, the counters carefully noted before leaving the board. Returning with renewed energy, we would soon sink again into an apparently everlasting struggle with no winner. The rules said nothing about games without end! And yet, as time went by, I sensed that this too was a life lesson. Not only was actual global domination the fervid, demented dream of insane dictators and deranged Bond villains, destined for continual disappointment; it was also the case that life itself was what physics had once declared impossible, a perpetual-motion machine of risk and reward, co-operation and conflict, victory and defeat. There were no final winners or losers in Risk, no matter what the rules said. And so, neither were there final winners and losers in that other game, the game of life—not to be confused with the Milton Bradley board game that predated Risk by almost a century but only took on its modern guise in 1960.

* * *

LIFE IS RISK. We all accept this—or at least say that we do. Most of the time, though, we act differently, as if we didn't know it. Perhaps worse, we often act in combinations of risk aversion and risk tolerance that are in sum irrational, creating second-order or meta-level risks that threaten the presumed sanity of the lower-level choices. Say someone limits intake of carbohydrates (aversion) because ingesting them is bad for their cholesterol but then drinks alcohol (tolerance) because they crave a sugar high? Result: a health condition far worse than just eating pasta. Or how about wearing a football helmet (aversion) but then hitting harder (tolerance)? Result: concussion and brain damage. Or, casting a wider community net, how about someone who bikes to work (community risk aversion) but doesn't wear a helmet (individual risk tolerance)? Result: costs to a shared health care system. And, in our current moment, how about self-isolating (aversion) but demanding children return to school (tolerance)? Result: potential asymptomatic super-spreaders.

All these outcomes are debatable, true, but they risk seeming like risk-related versions of people who drive across town to buy cheaper gas for their cars, with a net negative result.

Then there are variances within presumably common activity. One alarming set of concerns, as universities and colleges struggled with how, when, and whether to reopen to in-person teaching, was the generally higher levels of risk tolerance exhibited by people in their late teens and early twenties. But then there were uncomfortable factors such as statistics showing that college professors skew older than the general workforce, with almost a third over fifty. What is the smart decision concerning in-person teaching, even if everyone agrees it is desirable? In the most highly contentious example, wearing a mask during a pandemic has become comprehensively politicized, such that refusing to wear one, first compared to driving without a seat belt (personal expression of risk tolerance), is now commonly described as akin to driving drunk or with your eyes closed (community-based expression of risk aversion).

At least three human factors—sensitivity to the rewards of risk, lack of self-control when excited, and susceptibility to peer pressure—are demonstrably higher in young adults than in older ones. All combine to make any return to in-person post-secondary instruction, a form of pedagogy that many instructors consider clearly superior, highly risky.* "Not all adolescents are risk-takers, of course, and not all adults are risk-averse," a prominent psychology professor wrote. "But it's hard to think of an age during which risky behavior is more common and harder to deter than between 18 and 24, and people in this age make up about three-fourths of full-time American undergraduates."†

On the other side of this and other debates, nobody can ever eliminate all risk from life. You might isolate yourself, or wear a mask all the time, or douse every doorknob and incoming foodstuff with disinfectant. You might forswear all social events, restaurants, baseball games, and music concerts. You might do all this and more. And *still* there will be some threat to your health, wealth, and well-being that creeps inside your protective cordons. We must live; we cannot be zombies of caution—because this is to engage in a sort of living death, a death before demise.

Risk will not be denied, or controlled, or even always calculated with anything like reasonable accuracy. This starts with the most basic and most uncontrollable risk of all: being born. On a certain kind of possible-world meta-

....

* Mark Kingwell, "Let's Admit It—Online Education Is a Pale Shadow of the Real Thing," *Globe and Mail*, May 19, 2020.

† Laurence Steinberg, "Expecting Students to Play It Safe If Colleges Reopen Is a Fantasy," *New York Times*, June 15, 2020.

physics, what philosophers call modal realism, there are
infinite possible worlds imaginable and therefore in fact
real within the scope of what we naively call reality.
"Naively," because our supposed recognition of reality
and its limits is itself very narrowly limited by the paucity
of our perception and cognition: such "recognition"
almost always fails to capture how poorly even our most
useful models of reality—all of which are in some sense
false—match or describe even some small portion of the
real. (I will endeavour to limit the use of "scare quotes"
from this point on in the text; you could imagine every
single declarative sentence about the nature of the world
and our place in it as so enclosed.)

So: possible worlds. If there is an infinite number of
them—what is known as the *multiverse*—then it more
than stands to reason that at least some of them do not
include the statistically and historically insignificant
event of your birth. Or mine. Or indeed any specific event
or chain of events. My birth, and therefore my life and
consciousness, is a cosmically infinitesimal statistical
improbability. By force of larger numbers, I as the me I
experience myself to be should not reasonably be here.

And yet here I am, for all that. A scene from the television series *Hannibal* (2013–15) comes to mind. In the
narrative at hand, Hannibal Lecter, played by Danish
actor Mads Mikkelsen as a brilliant psychiatrist and con-
sultant, operating (and gourmet-cooking) before his
exposure as the well-known serial killer, speaks to his
therapist, the perennially beautiful Gillian Anderson.
"We have been here for one hundred thousand years," he
says. "In that time, one hundred billion lives have come
and gone." The mortal span is simultaneously trivial and

all-important. But that one hundred billion cannot be ignored, and certainly not subsumed by what G.K. Chesterton called "the small and arrogant oligarchy of those who merely happen to be walking about."* Chesterton meant that as an argument in favour of tradition; it is likewise an argument in favour of existential humility. You, too, will pass.

This thought of one's personal insignificance is, I think, at once both easy to accept and hard to reconcile, especially when we find ourselves, as we must, stranded in the present. Our current social and political realities are dominated by a very narrow time-slice of human possibility: proximate risks and questions about how to cope with them. Can we take a longer view, and hence slot risk into a more tractable place? I'm not certain: living beings always have a hard time assessing risk, and maybe an even harder one assessing cosmic time spans.

That is to say, we see the rational and literally inescapable force of our mortal limitations without, for the most part, being able to assimilate the existential implications of that force. I mean that we acknowledge death theoretically, but rarely with practical effect. It can be made to recede into dream thinking, a demon that is ever-present but also almost fictional in everyday life. This dual-stage denial is the main thread of those one hundred thousand years of human existence. Strangely, given its ubiquity, *we are bad at being mortal.* Hence *both* theistic subservience in its various forms *and* the rejections thereof in atheism, agnosticism, or skepticism. All of these are attempts to game the mortal system by dint of belief or its diametrical

....

* G.K. Chesterton, *Orthodoxy* (New York: John Lane, 1908), ch. 4.

opposite. But the system will not be gamed, or assuaged, or evaded. Indeed, the baseline multiversal thought—there are so many possible worlds, and yet so little actual time for each of us in any of them!—generates a host of strange insights about the dominating role of contingency. I mean that not just in human affairs—where we have long tried to school ourselves on the risks of risk—but in the very idea of the world itself. There is no world, and (to quote Sarah Connor in the *Terminator* franchise) there is likewise *no fate but what we make.*

Okay, fine. But how does that phrasing of reality help us, exactly? Well, let us attempt a little conceptual breaking down (if not a breakdown in the psychotic sense).

If you think the high-risk event of your own existence on this particular mortal plane is a long-odds dice roll, just think of how much slender probability is involved in the existence of anything at all. Physicist Alan Lightman, in an essay about the theoretical physics behind the concept of a multiverse—as opposed to the philosophical theory of modal realism, the metaphysical notion found in Leibniz, among others, of many possible worlds—said this: "While challenging the Platonic dream of theoretical physicists, the multiverse idea does explain one aspect of our universe that has unsettled some scientists for years: according to various calculations, if the values of some of the fundamental parameters of our universe were a little larger or a little smaller, life could not have arisen."

How so? Well, just think of the unlikely nature of finding the basic building blocks of biological life in one planetary stew. "[I]f the nuclear force were a few percentage points stronger than it actually is, then all the hydrogen atoms in the infant universe would have fused with other hydrogen atoms to make helium, and there would be no hydrogen left," Lightman notes bluntly. "No hydrogen means no water. Although we are far from certain about what conditions are necessary for life, most biologists believe that water is necessary. On the other hand, if the nuclear force were substantially weaker than what it actually is, then the complex atoms needed for biology could not hold together."*

Leibniz notoriously claimed that there was reason to accept that this world of ours was the best of all the possible ones—a doctrine extensively lampooned in the picaresque proto-novel *Candide* (1759) by François-Marie Arouet, known as Voltaire. Lightman and other recent physicists give us reason to doubt the statistical probability of even one very imperfect world. But, you might reply, here we are! But are we, or is this perhaps an elaborate simulation or a kind of board game played by higher-order entities? These world-shattering doubts are another long thread in the tapestry of philosophical thinking. The good thing—the saving grace—is that our own sense of purpose within this world seems unimpaired by all possible doubts, even if shot through with uncertainty whenever we pause to think deeply. We still experience ourselves, despite both physics and metaphysics, as *free agents of choice*—however tempest-tossed we might be. This is good.

But (there is always a but in philosophical argument) even here, where freedom of the will seems reasserted, *fate* is revealed as what some people would call a weasel word. Does it mean merely and tautologically *que sera*

-----

* Alan Lightman, "The Accidental Universe," *Harper's Magazine* (December 2011), 36.

sera, whatever will be, will be? Or does it indicate an apparently unchanging and unchangeable future that must be engaged in battle? Sarah Connor's version of its invocation would suggest that fate is really just another word for the summed effect of our decisions and actions. And yet making those decisions and performing those actions is precisely where aspiration meets reality, where potential becomes actual—and we cannot control many of the variables in play, let alone all of them. We also know, at least since Sophocles gave us a vivid and violent demonstration of the point, that trying to outwit or out-run your prophesied fate may simply hasten it: the tragedy of *hubris*. *Everything happens for a reason*, people say, as if to reassure themselves. *It's all good*. These are sops for an undisciplined mind, as primitive and superstitious in the New Age way as anything that ancient Greek wisdom sought to explode through drama.

* * *

LIFE, IT HAS also been said, is a series of bargains with the future. True enough, since we perforce live in the present and have only anticipation and planning to guide possible outcomes. Except that these negotiations are not really *bargains*, they are *bets*—and ones whose odds are very rarely calculable even in abstract terms. If life were a game of chance, we would probably choose not to play: the chances are stacked in favour of the house and against the players. But we did not choose, we were chosen. Hence the centrality of risk in human affairs. The most significant thing about risk is how bad we humans are at accepting and digesting these baseline facts, or even the less science-fictional versions of them that pass for common sense. We are continually making errors in life choice because, among other things, we misread our interests, like Midwestern presidential voters. More profoundly, we are distracted by our cognitive affinity for pattern making and narrative construction rather than assessing probabilistic data that are easily available.

We know why our penchants for narrative and pattern are so strong: they helped us achieve the wispy sense of individual self, that mysterious continuity over time that underwrites and extends our physical existence as organisms in a sometimes hostile environment. Narrative selfhood may be an illusion, neurologically speaking, but it is—or is felt to be—a necessary one. Absent the *narrative centre of gravity*, as one philosopher has called it, we cannot negotiate life plans on even a small scale, let alone form communities, plan complex undertakings, build civilizations, and create the arts, sciences, and philosophies that sustain us in what appears, accurately enough, as a meaning-free universe—excuse me, multiverse.* Thus our insistence on the meaningfulness of life, at least the pursuit thereof, when a few moments of clear thought reveal a fairly banal insight: when everybody's somebody, nobody's anybody. The fineness of your aesthetic or scientific per-

---

* See Daniel Dennett, *Consciousness Explained* (New York: Little, Brown, 1991). To be precise, Dennett holds to a "multiple drafts" model of consciousness, without a central homuncular observer in the "Cartesian theatre" notion of singular consciousness. This view makes room, therefore, for modular distribution of mindedness. For a radical alternative concerning the coherence of self, consider Derek Parfit, *Reasons and Persons* (Oxford: Oxford University Press, 1984), part three. Parfit argues that the connection between present and future versions of myself is experiential, not metaphysical. It may be important to me, and to ethics and law more generally, but it is not underwritten by further facts beyond my recognizing and accepting the connection. This will turn out to be *extremely important* when it comes to personal risk assessment, naturally.

ceptions, the fullness of your emotional life, the many
nuances of memory that make you who you are—none of
these are respected by more than a few, let alone by history,
still less by the vastness of existence itself. The sad truth is
that our sense of mattering does not matter.

Add to this sobering realization the idea that we need
not be here in the first place and the flood of contingencies may become unbearable. The lucky accident of my
birth—if that is indeed how to style it—is simply that,
another roll of the existential dice. Leavening the stew of
happenstance with an awareness of our own finitude is
not usually an escape hatch here, though some existential
thinkers would have you believe some such thing. That is,
full acceptance of the total meaninglessness of life is
somehow itself an entry point into superior mean-
ing-making, where we take responsibility for our freedom
and pass on a joyful open-endedness to others in so doing.
The often-repeated insight about Nietzsche's nihilism, for
example, is that it doesn't so much claim the lack of
meaning in the world as celebrate the fact that all the
meaning there is in that world is of human origin. Huz-
zah! But this is, for all the exultation found in certain
philosophical writing, a tough pill to swallow.

No wonder, then, that many people have sought refuge
in larger, indeed universal fictions. If the sense of self is a
necessary illusion, essential for us to continue hanging on
to the monkey bars of contingency, how much more
potent might be an illusion of transcendent direction and
control. Divine meaning might be opaque to us, creating
the familiar problems of extra-human justice we know as
theodicy: Why, exactly, do bad things happen to good
people? Why is there so much suffering in an allegedly

God-created world? And why, at the same time, do the evil or merely bad and lazy manage to prosper? But these opacities are tolerable if there is a background belief in general direction *combined with* special-pleading claims of limited human perception and the necessity of free will. God's rough justice is all part of the plan; and the very idea of the plan is what we require to make it through the existential night.

I am caricaturing, in part because I have, in common with many people, entertained and rejected these flimsy sorts of solace. What strikes me here, when considering risk, is how often divine changeability is, as it were, factored into the many bets on future events we are forced to make in life. I will have more to say about this in the section on Luck, but for now, consider just one legal and conventional concept: *acts of God*. These are unforeseen events, of the sort that not even insurance plans may attempt to calculate. They are folded into our schemes of risk assessment and risk distribution precisely because we know that the world is not orderly or even totally consistent. Is a pandemic an act of God in this sense? Much of the blame laying that has dominated political discourse lately is that (a) people should have seen it coming more quickly; and (b) they should have taken better measures to control and limit its effects. A lightning bolt is an act of God, but standing under a tree during a thunderstorm is just a form of human stupidity.

Perhaps the best single book about risk, especially in its social dimensions, is Ulrich Beck's canonical work *Risk Society*, from 1986.* In this now-classic treatise, Beck

* Ulrich Beck, *Risk Society: Towards a New Modernity*, trans. Mark Ritter (London: Sage, 1992); originally *Risikogesellschaft: Auf dem Weg in eine andere*

notes how all societies are shot through with risk, and with human thinking—often ill-informed, mistaken, or superstitious—about the variable life chances we all experience on the mortal plane. Beck's analysis demonstrates, among other things, that we can best understand late-model society not as post-industrial, or postmodern, or even neo-liberal and globalized—though each of these descriptors is at least partially accurate.

Instead, he suggests that the omnipresence of command-and-control economies, which try to regulate interest rates, money supply, and the distribution of goods, have created an unprecedented level of social risk. When some aspects of this form of governance are then conjoined with allegedly free markets and much regulatory capture, the results are even worse. This hybrid system goes hand in hand with—in fact demands and depends on—a vast system of production and consumption, and fragile, often decadent or divisive cultural eddies such as what we now usually label infotainment, culture wars, or Twitter storms. We might add to this more recent developments in overreliance on technology, the offloading of human decision-making to machine-learning algorithms, and the near-total ubiquity of mediated life for most of the planet's population. The inescapability of screens and the time we spend on them has created a

Moderne (Frankfurt: Suhrkamp, 1986). See also Niklas Luhmann, *Risk: A Sociological Theory* (New York: De Gruyter, 1991). Luhmann claims, as Maso notes, that the concept of risk had no fixed meaning until the Middle Ages, if not later, with the advent of reliable probability mathematics—a point to which we will return. Maso is also, notably, more sanguine about the role of technology in a risk society, in part because of his readings of Plato and Aristotle. Even Beck, he argues, subsumes *risk* under *danger*, and so fails to see the total immersion in hazard that is a necessary condition of all human will, reason, decision, and responsibility.

historically unique situation where risk can no longer be reasonably contained or managed, and frequently not even understood.* The notion that technology—that combination of *logos* (science or reason) and *technê* (skill or craft)—is going to solve all of our risk-based problems becomes, increasingly, the central risky problem. That critique is presumed in everything that follows.

Call this *technophobia* if you like; I prefer *neo-Luddite commitment*. A phobia is defined as an irrational fear. Many of us have no fear of technology, only critical attitude. A principled skepticism about technological "progress" and "inevitability" is entirely rational, indeed essential. And the neo-Luddite knows you don't need to smash machines; it's far more effective to smash the ideology that views new machines as always justified, always good, and always necessary.

As the philosopher Stefano Maso noticed, analyzing the philosophical category of risk, the interface of *technê* with the world, mediated by the rational aims of *logos*, is what contributes to risk establishing itself as "the authentic soul of the Western world." But when *phronêsis* (practical wisdom) and *technê* (skill) combine, they are "the two most powerful means that the Western man has available" to achieve the following three things: (1) manage the situation of absolute uncertainty and risk characteristic of the basic human condition; (2) definitively transform insane *risk* into concrete "determined"

---

* For my own take on one part of this cluster of issues, see Mark Kingwell, *Wish I Were Here: Boredom and the Interface* (Montreal and Kingston: McGill-Queen's University Press, 2019). In this book I use traditional philosophical analyses of boredom to open a portal into even more searching reflections on "the interface," which is not limited to a given program, platform, app, or system, but rather indicates any mediating function that stands between mind and world, interpreting and exchanging one for the other.

danger—such determination being a kind of metaphysical sleight-of-hand, or cultural card trick; and (3) thus convert the ancient hero—even the tragic one—into the modern master of technique at the centre of a "rational" society, which is not rational at all but instead deluded about its placement in the universe.[*]

This history and its resulting set of presuppositions can be very hard to see from the inside of our various techno-environments, including what McLuhanites call the *mediasphere*. It is therefore never going to be entirely clear what implications these findings cast over near- or long-term futures. A central aspect of risk society is its systemic reach; it is the water in which we swim, and therefore, like consciousness itself, perhaps beyond our own attempts at comprehension. One conclusion that can be drawn, however, and that decisively, is that our bets are usually finite, and ill-informed. We can call cosmic nonchalance *God* if we like; but that doesn't change our helplessness in the face of uncertainty, or offer anything except bogus comfort concerning that very helplessness.

The language of betting offers many profound lessons about chance and necessity. This is so partly because gambling is *conscious* betting whereas most of human existence, excluding high-risk exceptions like entrepreneurship or extreme sports, is *semi-conscious* or even *unconscious* betting. Many people and many religions deplore gambling as a vice; and indeed it can become an addictive and self-destructive habit, the thrill of uncertainty matched with the very real consequences of

....

[*] All quotations from Stefano Maso, "The Philosophical Category of 'Risk,'" *Philosophy and Epistemology International Journal* 1:1 (July 2018).

failure. But if everything in life is a species of bet—which I contend is the case—then the corners of existence where betting is taken seriously as the activity in which we are engaged deserve our special attention.

So here are some linguistic markers that may be, like chips, cashed in later on in our contingent time together. When I *take a flutter*, what exactly is fluttering? If I *go all in*, am I abandoning all hope or reaffirming the reckless ignorance of all hope, that most radical and meaningful of human actions? If I *hedge my bets* or *lay them off*, am I trying to control outcomes or merely making side bets to minimize possible damage on the main game? When I say *all bets are off*, because things have got out of control, is that a confession of despair or an expression of reckless confidence?

Some other gambling elements may seem a little less obviously related to human risk, but only at first glance. Is a *flat-bet strategy*, where the player bets the same every time, a good idea? No, not usually. How about the so-called *D'Alembert System*, where the player adds one credit to the stash after a losing bet and deducts one after a winning bet? Is that a reliable way to go home happy? No, not usually, for a person or (say) a public health policy.[*]

....

[*] The system is named for the French mathematician Jean-Baptiste le Rond d'Alembert (1717–83). D'Alembert is better known in academic circles for having co-edited, with philosopher Denis Diderot, the original *Encyclopédie* (1751–72). The gambling system that bears his name is prey to what is known as the *gambler's fallacy* or *Monte Carlo fallacy*, namely, that the odds are changed by a given bet when in fact they remain constant. The simplest version of this fallacy is also the most common: the idea that a string of bad outcomes makes a good outcome more likely. But odds are governed by the law of large numbers, and only extended reiterations make the chances clear. Consider the flipping of coins as a primitive example: each result of heads does not alter the fifty-fifty odds that the next toss will also be heads. Compare here, by the way, the *Let's Make a Deal* paradox—not really a paradox at all—that dictates a good bet after one of three options is removed is to *change your original bet*.

Worse still, maybe, is the *Martingale System*, where the player doubles up after every loss. Not recommended, say the guidebooks.* A memorable warning against this "system" comes in a dark fiction by crime author Lawrence Block, who knew what he was talking about. In his novel *Lucky at Cards*, Block's first-person narrator, Bill Maynard, a former magician and card sharp looking for a big score, relates a visit to a lunch counter. "There was a men's mag on the rack with a cover streamer touting an article on how to beat the craps tables at Vegas," Maynard notes. "I picked up the magazine and scanned the article. It was one of those bonehead jobs pushing the old double-up system—you double your bet every time you lose, and eventually you come out a winner." Even if this works for a while, "There was only one little flaw. Sooner or later you were bucking the house limit and the casino had you by the throat. I put the magazine back and crossed over to the phone booth."†

Nobody is really lucky at cards; the title of Block's novel is meant to be ironic. Playing cards, whose origins lie somewhere in Tang Dynasty China or ancient Persia or both, were probably imported to Europe and then North America by the usual spice-dominated trade routes. The decks we know today, used in games and tricks and recreations, are legacies of a long history of chance and socializing. Cards can be tools, tricks, accessories, or souvenirs. They are related to the mysterious

....

* Folk etymology suggests that the name for this system comes from an eighteenth-century casino owner, John Martingale, who was thought to encourage its use among his clientele—to their gradual disappointment and his profit.

† Lawrence Block, *Lucky at Cards* (London: Titan Books, 1964; New York: Hard Case Crime, 2007), 111.

divinations of the tarot deck, of course, but they have also been used as currency, as in early Lower Canada, and as symbols of death, as in Robert Duvall's memorable appearance as an air cavalry helicopter commander in *Apocalypse Now* (1979, dir. Francis Ford Coppola), placing them on Viet Cong corpses.

The standard deck used in most games and casinos is the so-called French Style, with thirteen pieces each of the four familiar suits of hearts, spades, clubs, and diamonds—once known, if you want to win a dinner-table bet, as hearts, pikes, clovers, and tiles. You can play an almost infinite number of games with this array, notably blackjack (because of the numerical combinations under and over twenty-one) and poker (because of the hierarchy of cards). The cards make it interesting, and hence profitable, that over five cards flush beats straight, full house—or *boat*, if you're cool—is ranked between flush and four-of-a-kind, and the latter hand lies just below straight flush, itself second place to the mythical royal flush. Never draw to an inside straight, and think twice before you donk-bet on the flop.

Gambling legend has it that poker is the thinking man's game, where skill will win out over luck in a long-enough run. It is also, at its highest levels, literally and simply a man's game: 97 percent of players at any high-level table are male, according to one female winner, psychologist turned player Maria Konnikova. While acknowledging that poker rewards thought, she also observes the clash of randomness and character that makes the game so fascinating. Even the higher metaphysics here are marked by elements of chance. "The equation of luck and skill is, at its heart, probabilistic," she notes, in a reminder that all fancy-pants players should heed, even ruthless, Vesper-swilling James Bond.[*] As noted several times already but worth repeating: The cards, like the rules of chance themselves, have no stake in individual human aspiration. When you are dealt a bad hand, in life or in cards, you are in trouble. This is known in the game as getting garbage, junk, a fistful of nothing, or a hand like a foot. Good luck with that, playah!

Bill Maynard's big score in the Lawrence Block novel is not a card trick, or even a good poker hand played skilfully. It is, instead, a murder pact with a femme fatale—of course. It goes sour, to the point where Maynard arrives at one simple rule for life and risk both: *don't gamble.* That's good advice, except that sometimes you have to, even while knowing that the odds favour the house. Maynard manages to escape, with the nice girl rather than the dangerous dame, and returns to a simple life of doing magic tricks with cards. "In the movies every sucker gets an even break," he muses late in the tale, "which is wrong. Runyon had the real story—all of life is six to five against."[†] That would be Damon Runyon, of course, and the claim has been repeated many times, even as some writers claim to find it nowhere in Runyon's published work. But, in fiction as in life, don't bet against the house; the quotation does appear, in somewhat different form, in a Runyon story from his 1934 collection *Money from Home and Other Stories.*[‡]

....

[*] Maria Konnikova, *The Biggest Bluff: How I Learned to Pay Attention, Master Myself, and Win* (New York: Penguin, 2020); reviewed by Michael Paterniti, "How a Writer with a Ph.D. in Psychology Became a Poker Champ," *New York Times,* June 23, 2020.

[†] Ibid., 185.

[‡] Damon Runyon, *Money from Home and Other Stories* (New York: Frederick A.

It's worth documenting, right here, the etymology of the word *gamble*, the thing you should not do, even when you think the odds are better than six to five against. The word is related to *game*, naturally—which seems simple enough. But note the spurious contemporary distinction offered in some jurisdictions where *gaming* is legitimate but *gambling* is a crime. This is a theologian-level hair split: sometimes *gaming* implies an exercise of skill over a contest of mere chance; at the same moment, it sometimes also indicates an activity that is just for fun and not ill-gotten profit, which might make it compatible with certain fundamentalist Christian values. *Gaming a system*, meanwhile, remains a favoured activity of GPA-shadowing undergraduates, SEC-evading investors, and high-level politicians.

And, in yet another quarter, a *gambit* should never be confused with a *gamble*. *Gambiting*, with a different etymological root in the wrestling move of offering a leg in order to obtain leverage, means attempting to trip up your opponent. In chess, a gambit might involve sacrificing a pawn to secure a tactical, and maybe later strategic, advantage in the game at large. I might even burn a knight or a bishop to get to the heart of the game's matter. Since at least 1855 in English, older with variants in other

Stokes, 1935). Compare this note from a letter to the editor of the *New York Times* (May 3, 1992) sent by one Maxwell E. Siegel of Wantage, New Jersey: "William Kennedy writes that he searches in vain for the source of Damon Runyon's famous betting odds against, which are indeed six-to-five. In 'A Nice Price,' a story in *Money From Home*, a collection of Runyon stories, Sam the Gonoph and Liverlips hear from Benny Southstreet that the Yale rowing team is favored over Harvard's three-to-one, considered a nice price." Siegel then quotes the story: "'I do not know anything about boat races,' Sam says, 'and the Yales may figure as you say, but nothing between human beings is one-to-three. In fact,' Sam the Gonoph says, 'I long ago come to the conclusion that all life is six-to-five against.'" For the record, the Yales do not figure as Benny Southstreet predicts. Score one for Sam, and one more for Runyon.

tongues, a *gambit* or an *opening gambit* are considered good moves, canny plays. We are always wrestling with each other, and likewise with chance itself.*

So, then, when things perhaps go badly and you *tap out*, that means you've lost your ability to play, perhaps even to pay for things elsewhere, such as rent and alimony. And we all know, or we should, that the reliable money in all gambling is to be skimmed not from the bets but from the *vig*, or *vigorish*, or *juice*—which is commission charged on bets, like interest on loans. The house always wins, especially now that roulette wheels have a double-zero as well as a simple one, but the smart money is, and has always been, on the friction between human desire and human disappointment.

Legend has it that in 1655 mathematician and philosopher Blaise Pascal (1623–62), he of the famous Wager on God, invented the roulette wheel in an attempt to fashion a perpetual-motion machine. Instead, he bequeathed to the world one of the most entertaining and heartbreaking machines of chance we know. If this is all so, the innovation counts as a wicked and wry commentary on life. The motion of the wheel is not physically perpetual, but its dark allure surely is, spun each time with the cry *Les jeux sont faits*—literally, "the games are made," or the chips are down, the bets entered. Compare, here, the Latin phrase *alea iacta est*—"the die is cast," a remark attributed by the Roman historian Suetonius to Julius Caesar as he crossed the Rubicon on January 10, 49 BCE. And thus another idiom for mortal bets, decisively crossing that river into

....

* I explore this gambit trope more completely in the Introduction to Mark Kingwell, *Opening Gambits: Essays on Art and Philosophy* (Toronto: Key Porter Books, 2008).

either disaster or greatness. Back at the wheel, meanwhile, the partner cry is invariably *Rien ne va plus*—no
more bets. Until, that is, the next spin ...*

Pascal understood the laws of chance better than
most. The celebrated Wager, put simply, is this: if you
stack a finite amount of human happiness generated by
living an amoral life, plus the possible infinite suffering
of damnation, against the possible infinite happiness of
salvation, plus the finite unhappiness of obeying God's
directives, the choice should be clear. It is, he insists, not
a matter of reason: we accept the conditions of uncertain
knowledge, and this is not a proof of God's existence. But
since we must bet, the choice to act with belief is a better
one given the clash of finites and infinites. Indeed, this is
known in decision theory as a *dominating* choice under
conditions of uncertainty.

The Wager can be gamed, naturally, if your particular
theology allows for a deathbed conversion, as some traditions of Christianity do. I could bet on disbelief for
now, and so max out my amoral happiness on this Earth,
and then switch bets at the last minute in order to be
welcomed into Heaven. In fact, some traditions rank
converts as even more welcome than routine and lifelong
believers. Score!

Anyway, that's for the future, yours or mine. In the
time before that, there aren't exactly loan sharks or vigorish on human aspiration, understood in its most general

....

* For completists and philosophy nerds: In 1943, Jean-Paul Sartre wrote a play,
later the screenplay for a film called *Les jeux sont faits* (1947, dir. Jean Delan-
noy), which was entered in the Cannes Film Festival. It is a political
fantasy-thriller, if that makes any sense, about betrayal and bargains in the
afterlife; as such, it has often been compared to Sartre's famous 1944 play
Huis Clos (in English, *No Exit*).

sense. Nobody but the Grim Reaper calls in your biggest bet. But there are plenty of sharks and enforcers, and schemes of compounding interest, to go around at lower levels of life-complexity. Beware the life bet that not only has long odds, and a big buy-in, but also carries long-term usury charges: the bets that keep on taking. We are not very good at calculating life odds, any more than we are good at doing math in our heads when embroiled in the heat of the casino floor.

Accepting that life is all about risk is the first cognitive step. The next steps are about how cognition, assuming we can achieve it, meets circumstance and the event-horizon that is the creeping, inevitable, unknowable future. To be very clear: time is decidedly not on our side in the probable multiverse. We have simply been delivered here willy-nilly—*thrown* into being and time, as a Heideggerian would say. Nobody asked us whether we wanted to be born: the disgruntled teenager's routine lament. But given that we are here, how can we make the most of it? Let's try to be good players, smart bettors, savvy calculators of the odds. The house will always win in the end—that's what the house does—but maybe we can scrape together a few winning hands or rolls along the way.

Put your money down, friends. You can't win if you don't play. And—what the lottery ads don't say—you're going to lose by not playing anyway. So you might as well throw caution to the winds, throw down, throw the dice—in short, *throw throw throw*.

2. Luck

"LUCK BE A lady tonight," Frank Sinatra sang in a 1963 record, and then again in 1965. The song was written a decade earlier, by Frank Loesser, and had already been performed by Robert Alda, Jack Jones, and Marlon Brando in the film version of *Guys and Dolls* (1955). Later versions would feature Barbra Streisand, Chrissie Hynde of the Pretenders, Brian Setzer of the Stray Cats, and Dee Snider of Twisted Sister, if you can believe. The lyrics are, as everyone knows, a lover's plea to the fickle mistress of chance, otherwise known as the goddess Fortuna. Lady Luck is very unladylike in her sudden bolting from presumed swains, unmannerly and unmanning. Prayer looks like the only option. Later verses feature further tropes of her inconstancy and betrayal, including wandering the room in search of other escorts and (my personal favourite) blowing on some other gambler-guy's dice. No, a lady doesn't blow like that!

Luck features in many popular songs, which I won't attempt to catalogue here. One of my favourites, though, is a 1967 blues standard by Albert King called "Born Under a Bad Sign," which includes the immortal (and repeated) line that if it wasn't for bad luck, some people wouldn't have any luck at all. The lyric, and the sentiment, has proved so universal that the song has been covered by everyone from blues legend Ray Charles to Eric Clapton and Ginger Baker of the mid-1960s English rock band Cream.

Luck is the great unknown in the world of risk, something that for some people simply doesn't exist except as a seductive fantasy, even as it is, for many others, the great spinning wheel of fortune's turn. From Machiavelli's political warnings and the tarot deck's forebodings, all the way to Pat Sajak and Vanna White on that forgotten but not gone game show, Fortune's random ups and downs can seem to dominate human life. (Television's wheel of fortune, meanwhile, when it comes to renewed seasons and sequels, spins just as capriciously as any other, yet game shows have proven almost as durable as soap operas when it comes to this windmill game of entertainment.)

Thus Hamlet's tortured reflection on whether it is all worth bearing:

> To be, or not to be, that is the question:
> Whether 'tis nobler in the mind to suffer
> The slings and arrows of outrageous fortune,
> Or to take Arms against a Sea of troubles,
> And by opposing end them: to die, to sleep;
> No more; and by a sleep, to say we end
> The heart-ache, and the thousand natural shocks
> That Flesh is heir to? 'Tis a consummation
> Devoutly to be wished.[*]

....

[*] William Shakespeare, *Hamlet* (Act 3, Scene 1), from the modernized First Folio.

Except there is a *rub* coming: the only thing potentially worse than a star-crossed life is a death where misfortune is erased along with consciousness. The deep paradox of the famous soliloquy is that the Prince of Denmark is not really facing a *choice*: the unknowable afterlife and the unknown future are alike versions of Shakespeare's "undiscovered country." Of course they are!

Speaking of Vanna White, and so running from the sublime to the ridiculous, who can forget—actually, most people can, but bear with me—the spot-on send-up of her vacuous, toothy-grinned spinmeister presence as voiced by Frank Gannon in his tribute essay "Vanna Karenina"?* As the narrator of Vanna's mundane tragedy notes: "Greed, mendacity, really bad taste in clothes, bad spelling, she had seen it all." Yes, she had—and so who could blame her if she sought desperate existential solace in flinging herself from the platforms of fame and fortune? In Machiavelli's brutal universe, as we know to our alarm, fortune's wheel turns like a hangman's engine, raising us up only to cast us down when conditions, or even weather and hygiene, rain on our parades. On television, it's a matter of spelling out well-known phrases for four hundred dollars a pop.

The great Irving Berlin song allows that dancing cheek to cheek can dispel the cares that hung around me through the week, making them seem to vanish in the same way as a gambler's lucky streak.† But there is no such thing as a

....

* Title essay in Frank Gannon, *Vanna Karenina* (New York: Viking Press, 1988).

† Irving Berlin, "Cheek to Cheek" (1935), written for Fred Astaire and Ginger Rogers, in the screwball musical comedy *Top Hat* (dir. Mark Sandrich, 1935); reprised in, among other films, *The Purple Rose of Cairo* (dir. Woody Allen, 1985) and *The Green Mile* (dir. Frank Darabont, 1999). Worth noting, perhaps, is that Astaire plays a gambler character called John "Lucky" Garnett in

streak like that; there is just delusion piled upon delusion. Luck is not a lady, tonight or any night; streaks are imaginary, given how odds really work. Luck is indeed a bitchy goddess, like her cousin Success, and has been called lots of other misogynistic names: a harridan, a temptress, a scold, and a dominatrix all in one. We can spare a moment here to note the patriarchal logic by which Fortune and Luck are almost always conceived as female ...

Men are statistically proven to be two times more likely to gamble than women, and seven and a half times more likely to have a betting problem or addiction—yet another of those population-dividing risk factors we can't fully control.* Dostoevsky's neglected 1866 novel *The Gambler* is perhaps the paradigm here, with some modern updates in fiction and film.† There are certainly some female problem bettors, not least the character Linda Howard as played by Julie Hagerty in *Lost in America* (1985, dir. Albert Brooks), who gambles away the coveted family "nest egg" of an upper middle-class couple seeking a comfortable retirement.‡ Then, in a famous *Simpsons* episode, Homer's long-suffering wife Marge becomes obsessed with local casino action, and falls prey to a creeping, monstrous addiction. "The only monster here is the gambling monster that has enslaved

---

another pairing with Ginger Rogers, maybe even better, namely *Swing Time* (dir. George Stevens, 1936).

* Chris Hemmings, "Why Are Most Problem Gamblers Men?" BBC *News*, February 13, 2019.

† Fyodor Dostoevsky, *The Gambler* (Russian, *Igrok*); loosely adapted to film as *The Great Sinner* (1949, dir. Robert Siodmak), with Gregory Peck, and *The Gambler* (1974, d. Karel Reisz), with James Caan.

‡ Best lines: After forbidding the use of "nest egg," Brooks's character David Howard rants: "If you are in a forest, that bird lives in a *round stick*. And, and, you have *things* over easy with toast."

your mother!" he declaims to a distraught Lisa. "I call him *Gamblor*, and it's time to snatch your mother from his neon claws!"*

Gamblor! All problem gamblers are addicts of a kind, if not always clinically so, but women with this form of impaired self-control are invariably seen as mad or bad or both. The male gambler, by contrast, can cut a kind of romantic figure, from the casual-seeming aristocrats featured in Thackeray's *The Luck of Barry Lyndon* (1844, source for Stanley Kubrick's brilliant 1975 film starring Ryan O'Neal and Marisa Berenson), insouciantly waving off a heavy loss, to the gun-toting anti-heroes of pretty much any western book or movie you care to name.

Kenny Rogers's cheesy country-pop crossover megahit of 1978, "The Gambler," strikes all the false, world-weary notes of the latter trope (lyrics by Grammy winner Don Schlitz). Most people remember the chorus about holdin' or foldin', whether to walk away or run, but the verses tell a hoary tale of two old guys on the proverbial train ride to nowhere, whose shared boredom gives way to an advice session, with flinty wisdom swapped for cigarettes and whiskey (what else?). The best lines are in verse three after chorus repetition one, where the cruel play of poker hands, both good and bad, forces the existential conclusion that a gambler's best hope is to die in his sleep. This is no simple risk taken in Havana; not even Warren Zevon's lawyers, guns, and money can get you out of this lifetime venture. That sententious nostrum, delivered as the old gambler fades off, breaking even with life at last, prompts the singer's conviction that this mortal outcome

* "$pringfield (or How I learned to Stop Worrying and Love Legalized Gambling)," Season 5, Episode 10 (Episode 91 overall).

is an ace worth keeping. Now let's have three more reps of that chorus, Kenny!

Luck is not quite the same as karma, the idea that future desert follows past actions, which is more like some conceptions of fate. Nor is luck synonymous with kismet, that other cognate notion that embraces ideas of destiny and fate. Luck is about chance, not destiny, and that is why it prompts so many superstitious and fearful responses. It is the most existential of extra-human forces, the one that is, if taken absolutely seriously, about *a lack of* governance and control. So pervasive and perverse is the logic of luck that many people consider wishing someone "Good luck" invites bad luck, and so they substitute a wish for a broken leg, good hunting, or tight lines instead. But be careful: *post facto taking back* of the over-hasty wish of good luck is, for the afflicted, only to double down on the bad kind. Do not go widdershins (counter-clockwise) through a churchyard, do not step on the sidewalk cracks, beware of black cats walking before you, and never, ever walk under an open stepladder. Duh.

"Although not all scholars are willing to recognize it," Stefano Maso writes, "'risk' is a real philosophical category." This may seem obvious, but Maso is making a serious and wide-ranging argument, as noted already, concerning how we misunderstand risk at a very basic conceptual level. We often use the term *risk* too loosely and without paying attention to its nuances—a task that philosophy in its category-clarifying mode can help with. More specifically, he investigates the terrain of Greek tragedy to understand how risk becomes reality, in Sophocles or Aeschylus but also in ordinary life. When Oedipus attempts to evade his foretold fate and so ends up only hastening it, that can certainly be ascribed to *hubris* or *hamartia*—the tragic flaw in each of us, even the greatest of us.

But more cosmically, we should note that such traits of arrogance or limit are *tragic* only when we fail to recognize how they clash with fate. When Icarus flies too close to the sun, melting his wondrous wings, is that fate? Yes and no. It is arrogance meeting circumstance, at once explicable and instructive. Do not tempt the gods of chance, or physics. No wonder the ancient Greeks viewed chance as fickle and untameable, a force lying beyond reason—hence their somewhat paradoxical fondness for lotteries and divination.*

"[I]t is necessary to distinguish risk from danger," Maso continues. "The danger is something defined and arranged by reason. So we can face it and we can defend ourselves against it." By contrast, "risk is in the background: it remains beyond rational awareness. The analysis of the etymology of risk leads us to the Arab-Byzantine era." I wonder if you saw that last move coming? I kind of did and kind of didn't—no odds offered on which. But here's the kicker: "The Greek language instead possessed the word *kindynos*, in which the thing or action you want to experiment is probably hidden." That last sentence is not exactly in good English syntax, but we take the larger, indeed global point: "risk and courage are frequently combined" and "the essence of Western civilization" can be caught "in the game between risk and reason."†

* I explore the political dimensions of *casting lots* in "Throwing Dice: Luck of the Draw and the Democratic Ideal," *PhaenEx* 7:1 (Spring/Summer 2012): 66–100; reprinted in Mark Kingwell, *Unruly Voices: Essays on Democracy, Civility, and the Human Imagination* (Windsor, ON: Biblioasis, 2012).

† Maso, "The Philosophical Category of 'Risk.'"

Maso is an attentive etymologist and also, partly as a
result, a good philosopher of risk. As noted already, he
relates risk to the Platonic account of *technê*, which is to
say crafting with skill, and Aristotle's notion of *phronêsis*,
understood as practical wisdom or good situational judgment. He then folds that combination into extant notions
of destiny and fate, of the kind that Sophocles had
already advanced to his enthusiastic Greek audiences.
This last move benefits from a theoretical boost from
Aristotle's own investigations of *catharsis*, the dramatic
staging and thus venting of fear and pity, in his *Poetics*.
But the Arabic root *rizq* is more resonant than these
Attic-Greek inheritors of ancient Arabic language and
thought. The Greek-Byzantine derivative *rizikòn* of the
even older Arabic makes the point clear: it alludes to the
silver paid to a mercenary soldier, the silver of proverbial
bribery, as in the thirty pieces used to turn Judas against
Jesus, or the silver that must cross a palm before business
can be transacted.

In French, the Latinate word for silver, *argent*, simply
means money, as in Émile Zola's 1891 novel *L'Argent*, a tale
of a bankrupt former financier banking his meagre means
on a get-rich-quick scheme. From the earliest linguistic
roots, in other words, risk has conjoined money, danger,
contract, and some kinds of courage. *Rizq* also means, per
the Koran, providence or sustenance—something
bestowed by Allah under his name Al Razzaq, the Pro-
vider. Divinity and prophecy are never very far away from
human bets, bargains, and bestowals.

Kindynos, for the record, gets very little traction on
contemporary search engines, but it can be traced back to
Greek-language sources for, among other things, the King

James Version of the Bible, known to us textual conservatives and doctrinal liberals as the KJV, where it is found in Paul's epistles to the Romans (8:35) and Second Corinthians (11:26), and usually translated as *danger* or *peril*. Saint Paul, who knew a thing or two about risk, having been knocked down from his horse on the road to Damascus, was aware that perils lie on every road—including the road to faith, for those who accept such a path. Faithful or not, there is risk on every road: "In journeyings often, in perils of waters, in perils of robbers, in perils by mine own countrymen, in perils by the heathen, in perils in the city, in perils in the wilderness, in perils in the sea, in perils among false brethren."

False brethren are, by definition, lurking everywhere—that's just what they do! This combination of pervasiveness and perversity is perhaps why luck and risk keep *showing up* in human thinking and planning, like the proverbial bad penny that is one of its talismans. The bugbear of luck, usually bad, is a trope of life's bad dice rolls almost as ineradicable as the notions of God's will or divine intervention. Indeed, the two concepts—God and luck, the divine and the dicey—seem often to come conjoined, albeit not very coherently. Let us explore this distinction further.

* * *

"GOD DOES NOT play dice with the universe," Albert Einstein is supposed to have said. The odds on whether he did actually say this, and what he meant by it, are hard to calculate. In a 1926 letter to colleague Max Born, published in 1971, Einstein wrote, "*Jedenfalls bin ich überzeugt,* *daß der nicht würfelt.*"* The claim notably does not include the notion of God, but rather implies an unnamed "he" or "it" (*der*) that does not roll dice (*nicht würfelt*). Moreover, Einstein is responding to what he sees as an unjustifiable probabilistic fatalism creeping into the so-called Copenhagen interpretation of quantum physics being advocated and popularized by, among others, Niels Bohr and Werner Heisenberg. (The disagreements and personal relations between these two geniuses are explored in Michael Frayn's superb 1998 play *Copenhagen*, set in the Danish capital in 1941, when the two met.)

Einstein, then, is not making a theological claim, or even really a cosmic one. He is challenging an overreliance on unexplained probabilities in a very technical corner of physical science, where such a lack of explanation is—or might be—considered a fault or shortcoming. "God does not play dice" has very little, if anything, to do with dice or, as it happens, with God.

But the popularity of the sentiment, which Einstein repeated somewhat uncritically in the years after writing this precise letter to Born, makes it abundantly clear that people enjoy grappling with the idea that a divine entity might (a) indisputably exist and (b) control *or not* the particular goings-on of the terrestrial plane beneath. From here we are but a few short steps away from the ancient Greek notion of fate. Oedipus encompasses his doom precisely by trying to forestall it, because that is what the gods will. Less dramatic and more irritating versions of fate might include the dopey reassurance, already noted, that everything happens for a reason or the arrogant

* Albert Einstein, letter to Max Born, trans. Irene Born, *The Born–Einstein Letters* (New York: Walker and Company, 1971).

superstition of the baseball player who crosses himself before every swing of the bat and then points to the heavenly skies when crossing the plate after a home run. Feh.

Consider, though, how situations beyond the trivial might inspire a certain kind of divine fatalism. No sane person would allow that the supreme entity has time to pay attention to baseball games, or to guiding the actions and outcomes of low-run corporate workers, but those in the midst of war and death often feel more poignant versions of what we must call *the fate conundrum*. Logic dictates that it is not about God, or gods, but luck is a much harder master to understand, even more than the most fickle and theodicy-defeating deity.

There is, by definition, extreme and unpredictable danger in battle. War is all about risk, as my board game adventures showed in a very, maybe extremely non-threatening manner. It is no surprise that soldiers become addicted to talismans and habits that they believe, irrationally, will carry them through conflict: having tight puttees or being squared away (see, for example, Paul Fussell's heartbreaking accounts of war in the South Pacific) or carrying rabbit's feet, vials of holy water, and supposed relics.*

I think often of my late friend Alison Gordon, a ground-breaking female beat reporter covering major-league baseball for the *Toronto Star* in the 1980s, telling me how many of these gifted athletes turned to Christianity for a putative rationale of their astonishing abilities

---

* Paul Fussell, *Thank God for the Atom Bomb and Other Essays* (New York: Blackstone, 1994). Soldiers once carried Celtic crosses or shards of the Holy Cross (fake or otherwise); these days they might load up with plastic toys or Saint Christopher medals. See Shea Butler, "Soldiers Find Comfort in Good Luck Charms," *DoD News*, November 15, 2006.

to earn money and adulation by catching and hitting small leather-covered spheroids. Some of them, to be sure, came from already very religious countries where Christianity was, among other things, a solace for the too-often benighted existence of colonial and post-slavery life for Blacks in the Caribbean. But others turned to born-again versions of faith as a way, it seemed to her, to offset the massive burden of sheer genetic luck that allowed them to live a life of riches and fame when they did not always experience a sense of worthiness from within themselves. Why me and not some other schlub from the same town or school?

There is no good answer to this except a measure of calm acceptance of chance's role in human life, combined with a keen critical eye for where solvable injustices may be attacked. Luck-generated inequities can be mitigated to some degree, as I explore in the next chapter; but to mitigate something, it is necessary first to acknowledge that there is a problem of inequity, and then to see that as a matter of justice-driven intervention. And we have proven ourselves, over and over, to be very bad at understanding the way fortune governs human affairs, large and small. Some things are minor but nevertheless contain social and political potential. Say I am an anti-social introvert who spends a lot of time reading and thinking about things. You are an extrovert whose daily interactions with other people, including physical contact such as hugs and shared offices, sustain you. We do not experience the effects of a pandemic lockdown in anything like the same fashion, and pretending that we *do* can load harm upon harm. Public policy must address everyone, but it needn't do so with no respect at all for the differences between persons. Risk tolerance and risk aversion are not fixed or simple properties, as we already saw, any more than sociability or its opposite.

One further lesson we must all strive to learn, if we have the wit to pay attention, is that even clever humans are highly unsuccessful at estimating risk, and worse still at incorporating any such estimates into their putatively rational decision-making and actions. Not surprisingly, there are entire fields of study driven by the irrational workings of the human mind as it suffers the hard bite of reality. The most important of these are actuarial science and economics. (Marketing and advertising follow close in the wake of these, but I lack the space to address them except by implication. Jonah Berger, Seth Godin, and Nir Eyal are all illuminating on those regions, especially when it comes to habit formation and viral success.[*])

In economics alone we must move not only from the macro to the micro, but also even more deeply into penetrating the unruly grey matter of human motivation and thought. Evidence is ample that the decisions we make, even or especially when we believe we are doing so cold-bloodedly and in the clear light of reason, generate all manner of pathological and self-harming results. The last distinction is important: if our self-interested acts merely worked to make things worse for others, that might be far-edge justifiable on grounds of pure selfish advantage. But the fact is that many of our attempts to maximize self-in-

....

[*] Jonah Berger, *Contagious: Why Things Catch On* (New York: Simon & Schuster, 2013); Seth Godin, *Permission Marketing: Turning Strangers into Friends, and Friends into Customers* (New York: Simon & Schuster, 1999); Nir Eyal, *Hooked: How to Build Habit-Forming Products* (New York: Portfolio, 2014).

terest only work to make things worse off for everybody, including ourselves. Sometimes, even more perversely, we make things worse for ourselves even as we unwittingly benefit others: the double whammy of self-defeat.

The classic example of selfish action generating collective defeat is Garrett Hardin's famous thought experiment of the tragedy of the commons.* In Hardin's analysis, inspired by some earlier cogitation about shared or public goods, the overuse demanded by an individual's goals works to destroy the shared advantage of having a commons in the first place. My overuse creates perverse incentives for you likewise to overuse, and hence we have a classic version of a race to the bottom. The more I seek advantage, the more you are competitively motivated to do the same. The ultimate result is diminishment and then, finally, elimination of the good that brought us to the scene in the first place, namely, available grazing land held in common.

....

* Garrett Hardin, "The Tragedy of the Commons," *Science*, December 13, 1968. Hardin's ecological analysis was inspired in part by an 1833 pamphlet published by William Forster Lloyd (no relation to Edward Lloyd, of Lloyd's of London), who also worked on the concept now widely known as diminishing marginal returns.

The much-quoted passage from his pamphlet is this: "If a person puts more cattle into his own field, the amount of the subsistence which they consume is all deducted from that which was at the command, of his original stock; and if, before, there was no more than a sufficiency of pasture, he reaps no benefit from the additional cattle, what is gained in one way being lost in another. But if he puts more cattle on a common, the food which they consume forms a deduction which is shared between all the cattle, as well that of others and his own, in proportion to their number, and only a small part of it is taken from his own cattle. In an enclosed pasture, there is a point of saturation, if I may so call it (by which, I mean a barrier depending on considerations of interest) beyond which no prudent man will add to his stock. In a common, also, there is in like manner a point of saturation. But the position of the point in the two cases is obviously different. Were a number of adjoining pastures, already fully stocked, to be at once thrown open, and converted into one vast common, the position of the point of saturation would immediately be changed."

As mentioned, though, there are irrational decisions that harm me even while benefiting you: being taken in by 99-cent pricing, for example, a trivial instance where the mind plays tricks on consumers' desires. Here, number play works to benefit the seller at the expense of the buyer, whose quick-fire cognition sees the large five, say, but ignores the 99-cent kicker that makes the de facto price a large, unseen six.

Economic analysis is rife with similar examples, even to the point of larger-scale, apparently deliberative choices that entail personal detriment: spending on apparent discounts in order to save money, for example, or the pervasive fallacy of sunk costs, otherwise known as sending good money after bad. My previous investment seems to provide a reason to continue or even increase my sacrifice, even when the evidence suggests (or demonstrates beyond all doubt!) that the debt is a bad one, never to be redeemed. The entire subset of economic thinking known colloquially as "freakonomics" includes large slices of analysis over just this sort of strange incentivizing—which, to be sure, can be motivated to good outcomes as well as bad.[*]

More closely associated with inner psychology are those analyses that show just how poorly our minds assess risk and reward—remarkably, in a way, since human evolution would seem to suggest that on a large time scale we have been pretty successful at reading fight-or-flight

---

[*] The ur-text is Steven Levitt and Stephen J. Dubner, *Freakonomics: A Rogue Economist Explores the Hidden Side of Everything* (New York: William Morrow, 2005); related thinking can be found in Richard H. Thaler and Cass R. Sunstein, *Nudge: Improving Decisions about Health, Wealth, and Happiness* (New Haven, CT: Yale University Press, 2008), which advocates social scaffolding to enhance positive choices under conditions of human psychological ineptitude. I discuss this last issue critically in Kingwell, *Wish I Were Here*.

situations. And yet this cosmic success has probably been won in spite of our shortcomings rather than because of our aptitudes. Regular courses at business schools and math programs show that exceptionally smart people are dumb when it comes to estimating probability in even very basic things.

The hoariest examples here are also the simplest. The first is the notorious coin toss. Everyone says they know, and accept, that the probability governing each toss of a fair coin is fifty-fifty. And yet people consistently react to what they perceive as probability-altering streaks. Ten tails in a row will almost invariably generate a confident prediction of heads on the next flip—and yet the fundamental distribution of chances has not altered. People also regularly respond more favourably to probabilities being revised downward rather than upward, even if the settled probability remains the same in both cases.

Suppose a bottle of wine has a 15 percent chance of being sour. But if I was first told that the chance was 10 percent, then I am significantly less likely to purchase the wine compared with being first told the chance of bad wine was 20 percent, revised to 15. (The swing here has been measured at levels as great as one-third more likely to buy up-revised possibly bad wine over down-revised possibly bad wine.)*

This is why it is always more persuasive—or at least action-inducing, since we are being fooled—to note upward revisions and numbers over downward ones. A product that is 9 percent fat is, presto, 91 percent fat free!

....

* Charlie Sorrel, "People Are Really Bad at Probability, and This Study Shows How Easy It Is to Trick Us," *Fast Company*, June 27, 2016.

If you ever feel yourself losing sight of probabilities in coin tosses, just recall the character Anton Chigurh, as played by Javier Bardem in the Coen Brothers film adaptation (2007) of Cormac McCarthy's 2005 novel *No Country for Old Men*. Chigurh, a psychopathic killer-for-hire, enjoys playing chance games with random strangers, perhaps because his paid jobs have made death so common and meaningless. Two scenes in the film use the conceit, to different ends but with an overall chilling effect. (Spoiler alert here.) In one scene, a hapless gas station attendant is forced to make the coin call, and chooses right. But only the audience knows that the game is deadly serious; the carhop thinks Chigurh is kidding—dramatic irony at its finest. The man survives. In the other scene, a Chigurh victim knows what the toss means, and refuses to call. She dies. You can't win if you don't play. But you can lose.

Let's be clear: the possibility of losing is *not* a reason to avoid play. Yes, if you play, you pay. You also pay for not playing, if that means abandoning a better world that might be of our collective making, even here, in the middle of a global challenge to what we thought life should look like. At the very least, we are right now in the middle of a historic opportunity, where our choices and decisions—our bets—have total mortal force. I want to see my next birthday; I expect you do too. Let's make that happen.

Speaking of birthdays, a simpler classic example of choice error is the so-called *birthday problem*, which preys on false intuitions about likelihood in populations. In a story recently related by a successful entrepreneur, a first-year business class is asked whether they are willing to bet five dollars against the chance that two people in a class of sixty-five have the same birthday. Students take the bet, over and over, and always lose: the first match is a fluke, they think, the second a wild anomaly. In fact, though, the probability of two people having the same birthday is over 99 percent as long as the group is fifty people or more. The five-dollar bills keep passing down to the smug professor at the podium.[*] Even at twenty-three people, the chances remain roughly fifty-fifty that two will have the same birthday. This is unarguable, yes, and apparently despite the fact that there are 365 days in the year![†]

The list of such scale-removing demonstrations goes on, offering to unmask the ways probability manipulates behaviour, which manipulation is often abetted—once more, both positively and negatively—by the graphic presentation of relative risks. A graph, for example, can be made to any scale, such that a small curve or line on a large version is made to appear like an unscalable peak on a smaller, higher-resolution one. Even without such potential adjuncts to mislead, people are just generally bad at numbers. They consistently report that 30 out of 1,000 is *more* than 3 out of 100, and regularly get confused over the rock-solid equivalency of those two (already identical) quotients with both the figure 0.03 and with the expression "3 percent." A lottery win is typ-

....

[*] Adam Taggart, "'The Birthday Problem' Shows How Terrible We Are at Estimating Probability," *Business Insider*, January 12, 2013.

[†] Logic and mathematics demand that 100 percent probability—the proverbial *lock*—is only secured with 367 people, guided by the pigeonhole principle (that is, every possible bet is covered). But the curve is so flat below that threshold that probabilities remain in the high nineties with just seventy people and do not reach the coin-flip stage until the twenty-three-people sample. This might well be the place to reference the sentiment attributed to both Benjamin Disraeli and Mark Twain, among others: "There are three kinds of lies: lies, damn lies, and statistics."

ically described by the size of the jackpot—$5 million, say—but the odds of winning are themselves one in almost 14 million when the game is a 6/49 format, and even then a jackpot winner only gets about 80 percent of the pooled fund. Powerball jackpots can be much bigger, beyond nine figures sometimes, but the odds there are close to a crazy-bad one in 300 million for the big win. That's a single winning ticket against almost the entire population of the United States.

According to statistical reporting, lottery odds compare very poorly indeed with other rare events, such as being struck by lightning (one in 1.2 million in any one year, rising to a frightening one in 15 thousand over an 80-year lifetime), being attacked by a shark (one in 11.5 million), and giving birth to identical quadruplets (one in 13 million). But hope dies hard when big numbers mesh and spark together with big desires. Let us recall with fondness the gap-toothed, bowl cut dolt Lloyd Christmas (Jim Carrey) in *Dumb and Dumber* (1994, dir. Peter Far-relly). When informed by the beautiful Mary Swanson (Lauren Holly) that his odds of ending up with her are at best "one in a million," Lloyd at first looks crushed but then slowly starts to smile. "So … you're telling me *there's a chance. Yeah!*"

As Cambridge University statistics professor David Spiegelhalter puts it, "Think about a big bath, fill it to the brim with rice. That's about 45 million grains of rice. Then take one grain of rice, paint it gold, and bury it somewhere in there. Then you ask people to pay £2 to put their hand in and pull out that golden grain of rice."[*] Well,

....

* Akshat Rathi, "A Cambridge Professor on How to Stop Being So Easily Manipulated by Misleading Statistics," *Quartz*, March 26, 2016. As Spiegel-

people will—because somebody wins, sometimes; and moreover, the one certain thing (as the ads say) is that you can't win if you don't play.

The sad fact—if it is indeed sad—is that improved knowledge of probabilities does not, in itself, suffice to change behaviour. In fact, meta-statisticians have suggested that the probability of better knowledge of probability changing behaviour is 30 percent or lower. Ha! Intuitions, however false, inaccurate, or downright irrational, are evidently stronger than reason. Twice a small number is still a small number; but don't tell that to the people who think they have just "doubled their risk" by eating a bacon sandwich or having a glass of wine while pregnant. (The cool-kid version of this point would probably be Bruno saying to Boots in Gordon Korman's *Go Jump in the Pool*, "Twice small potatoes is still small potatoes."*)

Statistics is a science both relatively new and massively misunderstood. A great deal of policy discussion is driven by it, as are the related fields of journalism and quantitative political science. A case study without numbers is no study at all, and every newsroom editor grows tired of reminding inexperienced reporters to "get the numbers." But numbers too often have only a deceptive patina of hardness and fixity. Their appearance, both in context and in presentation, should always be greeted

---

halter notes in this interview, one of his most reviled pseudo-rational claims is the much-repeated mantra, "Absence of evidence is not evidence of absence." This, he argues, is "always used in a manipulative way" to forestall further thought, argument, or investigation of evidence. There is always evidence; the job of sane, responsible people is to interpret that evidence sanely and responsibly.

* One of Korman's Macdonald Hall series of books: *Go Jump in the Pool* (Toronto: Scholastic Canada, 2003).

with skepticism. And no, I do not except the present work from this suspicion. This meditation on risk does not rely on statistics, let alone lean heavily upon their assumed authority; but I have quoted some numbers, and this might be thought inevitable when it comes to risk.

Because risk really is a numbers game, at its simplest a series of calculations over future possibilities and outcomes—not to mention over existing and future populations. The application of statistical analysis to human risk, including the formal study of actuarial science, was motivated in large measure not to eliminate or control risky outcomes, but to manage our expectations about them. The most obvious practical outcome of this is insurance.

* * *

WHAT, IN ITS essence, is insurance? It is a bet in the form of a contract made for payment. I give the insurer a premium, which is the nice name for a fee against potential misery. If all goes well, I never need to make a claim on a car wreck, a flooded house, or a devastating fire in my business's warehouse. I pay the premiums as financial tokens of security, purchasing peace of mind with my discretionary dollars. These fees are a net loss for me if my fortune is good, but most people reckon it's a good hedge on life's larger bets of uncertainty, malfeasance, acts of God, and my own or other people's stupidity.

With life insurance the bet and its hedges alter. I am certainly going to die, and that outcome cannot be forestalled, it can only be purchased as a potential future gain for someone else. Meanwhile, life goes on. We all hope we never find ourselves in the position of George Bailey (James Stewart) in *It's a Wonderful Life* (1946, dir. Frank Capra), where we might begin to feel that we are worth more dead than alive.

As philosopher Ian Hacking has documented, a great advance in understanding the very idea of *chance* was made possible only by the availability and thus potential study of good statistical data, including population numbers.* All the mathematical prowess in the world will not offer a good understanding of risk if we don't have good numbers to begin with as raw material. Interpretation of these, and of potential manipulations and deceptions, come only after the numbers are crunched. (I am leaving out of play here the obvious misinformation of falsified or fictional statistics.)

Actuaries and insurers can use the numbers, then, to make viable generalizations across populations and events, and thus calculate good premium-to-adjustment ratios. No insurance plan will ever be entirely immune to fraud: someone setting their own warehouse on fire, someone taking their own life while pretending it is no suicide, or—the plot device of many a film noir thriller— making the death of another look accidental in a murder-for-money scheme. Perhaps the most famous of these is *Double Indemnity* (1944, dir. Billy Wilder), which combines a conniving salesman (Fred MacMurray), a devious femme fatale (Barbara Stanwyck), and a canny claim investigator (Edward G. Robinson). The title phrase

....

* Ian Hacking, *The Taming of Chance* (Cambridge: Cambridge University Press, 1990). This book is considered a sequel or supplement to Hacking's earlier work, *The Emergence of Probability* (Cambridge: Cambridge University Press, 1975).

refers to a clause sometimes to be found in life insurance plans, which doubles the payout in cases of accidental death such as falling off a train—or *seeming to.*[*]

Modern actuarial plans are rooted not just in the data-gathering practices of the seventeenth century documented by Hacking, nor in the "emergence of probability," as he calls it, that resulted in advances in mathematics, especially calculus, and the logic of induction. The correspondence between Pierre de Fermat and Blaise Pascal is central here, moving the ancient notions of wild chance or fortune into a calculable terrain. Maybe even more significant is the use of chance-based mathematics as devices of command and control. Here, Hacking follows the insights of his great social-theoretical influence, Michel Foucault.

As Foucault had argued in his own work, mechanisms of social control emerge out of the historical changes undergone by institutions: clinics, prisons, bureaucracies. When such mechanisms are bolstered by the apparently solid findings of statistical investigation, a formidable structure of influence is deployed. Insurance itself may have developed as a way of offsetting across, spreading potential misfortunes through the population field of a

....

* There are dozens of books on actuarial science, including both technical and practical treatises. The best historical and theoretical survey of the field I know is Craig Turnbull, *A History of British Actuarial Thought* (London: Palgrave Macmillan, 2017). It runs a gamut from mathematical concerns rooted in the work of Blaise Pascal and Pierre de Fermat to fascinating accounts of the eighteenth-century notion of "equitable life," or prosperity sharing. The *British* part of the title should not be read too narrowly: Turnbull draws on sources from everywhere, including Continental and American cases.

See also Dan Bouk, *How Our Days Became Numbered: Risk and the Rise of the Statistical Individual* (Chicago: University of Chicago Press, 2015), which offers a complementary account of how American capitalism embraced and deployed widespread insurance schemes and risk offsets, often sold by travelling salesmen or drummers. The focus here is, instead of firms and compacts such as Lloyd's of London, the sovereign republican (capitalist) individual as the only guarantor of his or her own life risks.

firm like Lloyd's of London or amortizing danger via personal premiums; the darker side of this minimizing of risk is the reallocation of risk according to numbers.

Here we move from the relatively benign field of personal risk management into the sometimes alarming regions of social tracking and planning. The statistical analysis and emergent probability theory of the seventeenth and eighteenth centuries are the *early modern* versions of what would later evolve into the *high modern* control systems and military logistics of the nineteenth and twentieth centuries. The two modern modes of social control then become, in turn, the centralized corporate forebears of the agency-stealing *postmodern* soft-control mechanisms. These shady or even invisible mechanisms involve public-space surveillance, triangulating your shopping preferences and social media clicks, and maybe monitoring your computer's built-in camera or microphone.

So offer an abject welcome, citizens, to your algorithmic overlords! Even resisting having your picture taken without your permission—a personal risk by any reckoning—will these days be mocked as technophobia, superstitious primitivism, or misplaced vanity. But let us heed the prophetic words of Susan Sontag, written before Facebook, Instagram, or even widespread CCTV: "To photograph people is to violate them, by seeing them as they never see themselves, by having knowledge of them that they can never have; it turns people into objects that can be symbolically possessed. Just as a camera is a sublimation of the gun, to photograph someone is a subliminal murder—a soft murder, appropriate to a sad, frightened time."*

....

* Susan Sontag, *On Photography* (New York: Farrar, Straus, and Giroux, 1977).

Social control always requires social planning, and planning itself is worthy of concentrated study, especially in relation to potential risk and reward. Here I can offer only a few notes about plans and risk.

There is a Yiddish proverb that says *Der Mentsch Tracht un Gott Lacht*. The rhyme is lost in the standard English translation: "Man plans, and God laughs." That loss might itself be considered another tiny cosmic joke. The bigger joke is on us, because whatever your conception of God might be, the limitations and final futility of human planning are indeed mocked by the vast, inscrutable powers beyond us. That's life, people shrug, repeating once more that *it's all good*—the lurking and even more vacuous cousin to *everything happens for a reason*. Well sure, if by "good" and "reason" we mean something other than what can be comprehended by normal standards of benefit and ordinary capacities of human intelligence. We are back in the realm of disreputable theodicy.

In human affairs alone, planning is at best an undertaking only half-possible—that is to say, both necessary and doomed. "No plan survives contact with the enemy," Field Marshal Helmuth von Moltke the Elder is supposed to have said. It is a warning that every sagacious commander must remember. More accurately, Moltke said this: "No plan of operations extends with any certainty beyond the first contact with the main hostile force" (from his essay "On Strategy," 1871).* My own favourite condensation of this curb-your-enthusiasm wisdom is attributed to heavyweight boxer and convicted felon Mike Tyson: "Everybody has a plan until they get punched

---

* Helmuth von Moltke, in *Moltke on the Art of War: Selected Writings*, trans. Daniel J. Hughes and Harry Bell (New York: Presidio Press, 1993).

in the mouth."* Ouch. But then Robert Burns salves the wound a little, maybe, with his 1785 cosmic-insignificance poem "To a Mouse, on Turning Her Up in Her Nest With the Plough": "The best laid schemes o' Mice an' Men / Gang aft agley"—out of Scots into English that's "go oft awry," not nearly as good if you ask me. We are all revealed as "Wee, sleeket, cowran, tim'rous beasties."

So may fate grant me a simple plan—but let us hope it is not the tangled kidnap-murder-mayhem plot of the movie of the same name (1998, dir. Sam Raimi). There are no *simple plans*, only simple people who believe in them. One can appreciate anew why military planning is rich in warnings about unpredictable contingencies, the fog of war, and battle confusion. It is also rife with adages that reflect the reality of mortal risk. "Plan your dive, and dive your plan," frogman sailors like to say. That would be a good day, if the planned dive went as planned. More to the point might be that other military slogan, cited earlier, about two, one, and none. This piece of practical wisdom dictates, as we know, that you should always make sure you have a replacement, because your replacement is there to ensure that you actually *have* the thing that you *don't want to have* to replace.

A vivid and brutal version of this nostrum comes in a scene from Michael Cimino's Vietnam-era film *The Deer Hunter* (1978). The wedding party of friends go deer hunting, changing out of their tuxes into plaid shirts and down vests. One of them has no boots, and asks to borrow the spare pair always carried by Robert De Niro's character, future paratrooper and Russian roulette prisoner of war.

---

* Also the title of a 2016 album by jazz guitarist Charlie Hunter. Often revised in online memes to read "until they get punched in the face."

He refuses the loan. "Every time he comes up here, he's got no knife, he's got no jacket, he's got no boots." When his doofus pal complains, calling him "a fucking bastard," De Niro brandishes a rifle cartridge he is about to load. "You see this? This is this. This ain't something else. This is this." If anyone was ever in doubt about the title of this film, that single cartridge tells you everything you need to know. *This ain't something else. This is this.*

One might think of King Lear at this juncture, goaded by his daughter Regan to reduce his entourage of courtiers: "What need one?" she asks nastily. "O, reason not the need!" Lear thunders, in growing madness-addled vexation (*King Lear*, Act 2, Scene 4). *Superfluity*, he goes on to argue, is what raises us above the beasts, whether that means a few unnecessary henchmen or the gorgeous and fashionable but not warming clothing that Regan likes. (Lear is himself superfluous at this point in the action, had he but known it.)

And if we want to go even more gangster with useful planning adages, how about this one, quoted in (among other places) Quentin Tarantino's 1993 neo-noir thriller *True Romance*, uttered by Christian Slater doing his best Jack Nicholson impression: "It's better to have a gun and not need one, than need a gun and not have one." No doubt true, though that remains something I hope I never need to test out.

Planning is not constrained by its own awareness of limits, however, necessary though that is. In addition to known contingencies—contact with the enemy, somebody's fist, a rifle shot—there are unknown ones. We find ourselves in what has come to be known as Rumsfeld's Quadrant.

The former US Secretary of Defense, attempting to justify the invasion of Iraq in search of non-existent weapons of mass destruction, offered a notorious but incomplete epistemology. There were, Donald Rumsfeld said, three categories of knowledge: (1) known knowns, (2) known unknowns, and (3) unknown unknowns. The last category could not be anticipated, and hence the need for pre-emptive attack. As critic Slavoj Žižek has pointed out, though, that leaves one corner unarticulated: (4) *unknown knowns*, the invisible but operative presuppositions of all political ideology, the things we assume rather than defend. This would include, among other things, the presumption that armed invasion is a God-given right.[*]

At the far end of the spectrum of what can be known or predicted lie entirely unprecedented events that, however statistically unlikely, nevertheless happen, and often with disproportionate effect. In stock market lingo these are known as black swans and, like the unicorns that likewise stalk the market's collective imagination, they sometimes do appear.[†] We might be better off thinking of, if not anticipating, the fate of another bird, the Thanksgiving turkey. Per inductive logic, it has every reason to suppose that each new day will bring another episode of happiness and easy eating. But then, come some semi-arbitrary day in October or November, the axe falls, and the bird is the one providing the happy eating. Now *that's* contingency. This is this, bird-boy.

....

[*] There are many versions of this argument, e.g., Slavoj Žižek, "Rumsfeld and the Bees," *Guardian*, June 28, 2008.

[†] See, for example, Nassim Nicholas Taleb, *The Black Swan: The Impact of the Highly Improbable* (New York: Random House, 2007).

Insurance and planning, however meticulous, can never purchase true security. We all get punched in the face sometime, even if we're wearing a mask as we should.

Meanwhile, the selling of insurance, indeed the very idea of the insurance salesman, remains a standard if rather tired joke. The salesman is invariably seen as intrusive and unwelcome. You see one such gormless broker bothering Phil Connors (Bill Murray) over and over in *Groundhog Day* (1993, dir. Harold Ramis). There is likewise a famous *Simpsons* episode in which Homer dislodges a crayon that has been stuck in his brain, making him immediately smarter than average. But intelligence is painful, he finds, so he plans to re-insert the crayon so that he can fit into American society once more. As Moe the local bartender, doubling as a backroom surgeon, pounds the crayon up his nose, Homer says, "Extended warranty? How can I lose?!" Purchasing one of these *might* make sense for a used car, say, or an appliance. It is very dark humour indeed to consider it a good deal for what Moe calls "the old crayola oblongata."*

What started as a plan to aid humans in their risk, then became a plan to constrain and direct those humans to specific purposes and outcomes, now expires as a common cultural joke. How can I lose? Let me count the ways.

* * *

....

* "HOMR," Season 12, Episode 9 (Episode 257 overall). For a more extended discussion, see Mark Kingwell, "Crayon in the Brain: Machining Happiness in the Time of Homer," *Descant* 37:2 (Summer 2006): 68–87; reprinted in *Practical Judgments: Essays on Culture, Politics, and Interpretation* (Toronto: University of Toronto Press, 2002).

GIVEN EVERYTHING THAT has been said so far, it becomes obvious that the basic logic of all measures of prediction and control must be queried in existential terms—acknowledging that this adjective means different things not only in the wider world but even within this attempt at a fairly precise conceptual foray into risk. (See, for example, "existential risks" in a later section of the present work, which concern global scenarios of doom.) What I mean by "existential" here is simply the presumptive centrality of individual existence, otherwise known as selfhood, discrete consciousness, or personal identity.

Such selfhood seems so basic to our thoughts and feelings that it courts absurdity to question it. And yet this presumptive category is not nearly as central or as valid as we usually choose to believe. Modern insurance schemes, actuarial calculations, and planning regimes may be based on a kind of fictional discrete self—the self of legal personhood, let us say, underwritten by signatures and documentation and testaments—but the reality is far more complicated. Just on a risk level, there is actually no such thing as individual risk: all risk, regardless of my apparent focus or first-person interest, is a matter of sharing and offsetting. There is no such thing as a single-player game.* Even natural risks, as distinct from betting contests and schemes to divide shipping or other

....

* Possible exception to this assertion, offered by my esteemed colleague Peter King: seduction may be usefully characterized as "a two-person game with just one player" (Ninth Annual Symposium on Sex and Love, Philosophy Course Union, University of Toronto, 2013). The idea here is that only the seducer knows that there is a game afoot; that's what makes the game what it is, and he (usually, but not always, a he) is both the instigator and arbiter of the game. But without the seduced/seducible target person, there is no game at all. Obviously, this idea can then be noted as one of the roots of the designation (positive or negative, depending on circumstance and attitude) of somebody being a "player."

forms of liability, depend upon community and its potentials for failure. Natural hazards are only rarely zero-sum in the strict sense, but it is still obviously true that the aid or relief I receive therefore is something that cannot be received by anyone else.

Consider, then, pandemic risk as a natural hazard to communities. We saw already that Berlin's "negative liberty" argument comes into play here, with people assuming—often in direct defiance of science—that incurring their own individual risks is simply about their choices and freedoms. At the very same time, and sometimes from the very same people, we hear arguments that the only way to defeat a pandemic virus is through a combined program of mass vaccination and herd immunity. The enforced logic of the former (resisted even before the current pandemic, over flu and smallpox shots, by insane anti-vaxxers who think inoculation is a deep-state plot) and the harsh logic of the latter (we must let some suffer and die in order for the larger population to survive) are inherently *communitarian* rather than individualistic. In any herd, there are two fundamental tenets: (1) no individual is more important to survival than any other; and (2) the weakest are, fortunately or otherwise, the most likely to die.

Okay, I agree—very nasty, if true. But now consider the still more unsettling fact that the texture of your individual experience, your sense of being conscious and freely willing, is essentially irrelevant to the wider world. You simply do not matter as you; the best you can assume is that you matter as one piece in a larger community-based program of evolutionary survival. Even here, you are entirely fungible and therefore replaceable. You are not only not special, you're not even unique—despite what your inner voice of first-person narrative keeps insisting.

There are various philosophical versions of this deflationary insight. Some, like Richard Dawkins's notion of memes, argue that persons are just carriers of coded cultural messaging, vehicles of language and gesture.[*] Others, like the high-toned speculation of analytic philosophy, suggest that personhood is a made-up story, a necessary narrative to support life but with no grounding in external reality. Still others—and I would include myself here—seek at once to honour the sense of self and to expose its vulnerabilities to structural manipulation, externally generated desire, and harmful systemic goals. (The last include those of neo-liberal capitalism, which are actually in their effects actively counter-evolutionary.)

From this last possibility I derived the notion of what I labelled, in some previous work, *person casings*. The coinage was inspired by the final, post-apocalyptic section of Jennifer Egan's 2010 novel *A Visit from the Goon Squad*—goon squad being her vivid image for death and dying. You might say, per Mike Tyson: everybody has a plan, until the goon squad shows up. Here they come, for each one of us, sooner or later ...

In Egan's text, the narrator explains the idea of *word casings*: formerly meaningful usages that had become hollowed out or rendered risible through overuse and misuse. "Rebecca was an academic star," we are told. "Her new book was on the phenomenon of word casings, a

....

[*] Richard Dawkins, *The Selfish Gene* (Oxford: Oxford University Press, 1976). The idea of a *meme*, to which Dawkins gave a precise definition as a unit or cluster of cultural information conveyed through gesture or language, using persons as hosts the way genes use bodies, has been reduced to any Internet-borne bit of trendy effluvia or catchy hashtag. To which I say: #meh. (That one probably won't catch on.)

term she'd invented for words that no longer had meaning outside quotation marks. English was full of these empty words—'friend' and 'real' and 'story' and 'change.'" These were "words that had been shucked of their meanings and reduced to husks. Some, like 'identity' and 'search' and 'cloud,' had clearly been drained of life by their Web usage. With others, the reasons were more complex; how had 'American' become an ironic term? How had 'democracy' come to be used in an arch, mocking way?"*

Person casings, by extension, are husks of formerly robust individualism now reduced to not quite mockable emptiness. We are more like Gilles Deleuze's nation of control-society *dividuals* than we are individuals in the old liberal sense of self-guiding, choosing agents. We are not even disciplined, only controlled; we exist simply as bundles of references guided by outside forces, tracked and enabled by consumer software, reduced to predictable patterns; or we navigate the world as concentrated non-subjects, really just triangulations of surveillance and tracking technology, no more than the sum of our caught images.†

There is no unique individual nexus or core at work here, so the argument goes, certainly not a stable version of authenticity over time. There might not even be, to employ Daniel Dennett's attempt to forestall thoroughly deflationary arguments about selfhood, "centres of narrative gravity."‡ Such a narrative self-centre, in common

....

* Jennifer Egan, *A Visit from the Goon Squad* (New York: Alfred A. Knopf, 2010).

† I pursue these arguments at greater length in both *Unruly Voices* (Windsor, ON: Biblioasis, 2012) and *Wish I Were Here*. See also Gilles Deleuze, "Postscript on the Societies of Control," *October* 59 (Winter 1992): 3–7.

‡ Cf. Dennett and Parfit, discussed earlier (note p 53).

with any old-school or naive physical-mental one, was only ever notional at the best of times. It was a compromise between the stubborn sense of identity from the inside and awareness of the realities of the outside. Thus brain and mind were not linked so much as joined in an uneasy détente.

This compromise with physical reality is then represented and articulated as a host of ghosts, a cast of characters, the way the sum of mechanical and postural vectors can, for example, allow a high jumper to have her or his centre of gravity actually pass beneath the bar. Now, worse, this merely notional centre itself has been displaced when it comes to self-written narratives of personal identity. What if all the characters, like those in Luigi Pirandello's celebrated play, remain forever *in search of an author*? There is no author, just performance. There is no stable centre self, just responses to economic and political conditions.

This is a cage-rattling set of conclusions for all of us who live our everyday lives thinking we simply exist as individuals, and not deracinated or tempest-tossed, hollowed-out dividuals. Is all therefore lost to our sense of identity and planning? Are all risks both terminal and not actually directed at me—because there is no me, really? Well, alas, yes—in one important philosophical sense (at least according to me). At the same time, there is no reason, or no more reason than usual, to panic. You are here, and evidently conscious. Descartes was right about that. If the sense of self, of personal identity over time, is revealed in various philosophical ways to be a fiction, or a construct, it is nevertheless an unavoidable if not quite necessary fiction. We are not, or not yet, agency-free zombie-selves. We can choose, and act, and make our worlds better. That makes us another species of the ones who revive again and again in the face of death.

Zombies cluster and clamour everywhere on our shared cultural and political terrain. That's what zombies do; that's what they are. They want to eat brains, it's as simple as that. Even in this short text we have already encountered zombies as (at least) (a) the potential inhabitants of a future so risk-addled that real life is impossible *and* (b) the agents of a potentially viral apocalypse. Economist Paul Krugman, meanwhile, has been talking of late about (c) "economic zombies," meaning misunderstandings and brainless policy ideas that refuse to die, lingering to exert harmful effect.[*] We could even add (d) a fourth cultural resonance, drawn from a late June 2020 satirical tweet about conspiracy theories concerning the origin of the COVID-19 pandemic: "Any zombie movie that doesn't have hordes of people running towards the zombies to deliberately get bitten because they're convinced it's a liberal hoax is going to look pretty unrealistic now."

Ah, so funny because so true! In the pages that remain, I propose to do two things. First, I want to rescue our meagre sense of self from ideological, viral, and (some) economic zombie depredations alike. Second, I want to suggest that there is, perhaps contrary to intuition, a kind of bright future available to those of us who respond to the risk regime by accepting our status as post-apocalyptic entities—which is to say, philosophical zombies of a peculiar and resilient kind.[†]

....

[*] Paul Krugman, *Arguing with Zombies: Economics, Politics, and the Fight for a Better Future* (New York: W.W. Norton, 2020).

[†] My idea of hope-based post-apocalyptic revenants is not to be confused with

In short, there is a good way to be a revenant: rather than mindless, rapacious, and relentless, now mindful, spare, and appropriately existential.

....

the philosophical zombies used by recent academics to argue points about the redundancy of consciousness—though there is a connection between them that I cannot pursue at present. See, for example, David Chalmers, *The Conscious Mind* (Oxford: Oxford University Press, 1996). Chalmers's argument, much discussed, is that philosophical zombies—indistinguishable replicas of humans but without interior consciousness—are inconceivable, and hence mind must be more than merely physical.

3. Politics

DURING THE LATER parts of the 1980s, I lived in the New England university town of New Haven, Connecticut. New Haven had a bad reputation that has not been much countered by more recent history. Once a prosperous small-scale industrial city, with a booming carriage trade and an emergent industrial base in, among other things, the Winchester Repeating Arms Company—manufacturers of the massively successful M16 rifle, standard military issue—the city had fallen on hard times.

Nevertheless, the lively local theatre scene was intact, and the town was, even late in the century, regarded as a place where would-be Broadway hits would have their trial runs. See, for example, key scenes set in a hotel near the town's Shubert Theatre in *All About Eve* (1950, dir. Joseph L. Mankiewicz), in which creepy Addison DeWitt (George Sanders) tries to dominate inveterate climber Eve Harrington (Anne Baxter) with his knowledge of her shady past. The Shubert was still a powerhouse in the 1980s, as was the more radical Long Wharf Theatre, creative home of Black playwright August Wilson.

Wilson was, in his way, more emblematic of New Haven than all the white-boy college stories that were set there in young-adult novels of the early twentieth century: *Frank Merriwell at Yale* (1903), *Andy at Yale* (1914), *Stover at Yale* (1912), and so on and on. These fantasies of white athletic virtue, extremely popular for decades, depicted a bucolic college town full of good talk, hard-fought football games, and the almost irresistible temptations of drink, tobacco, and actresses. By the 1960s, the city had experienced, if not assimilated, the effects of the Great Northern Migration. It was, outside the castellated walls of the university, largely a Black city and the rest of us were just visiting.

This could be hard to see because of the kind of unspoken segregation that is common in cities from Boston to Detroit to Chicago to Los Angeles. What I mean is that it was understood that there were places you did not go. No actual walls demarcated the neighbourhood boundaries, but they were fixed and policed all the same. Do not walk too far up Elm Street or Whalley Avenue, past the student greasy spoons. If you go to a hockey game at Ingalls Rink, don't cross Mansfield Street or Winchester Avenue. Be careful of Columbus Avenue and Martin Luther King Jr. Boulevard.

New Haven had, at the time I lived there, the highest per capita murder rate of any city in the United States. I experienced no violence myself, but I do vividly recall being made aware of the intersection of race and class over and over again. A young Black man approached me one day when we were both waiting in line at the local Federal Building, trying to secure social security numbers. He needed help filling out the form because he couldn't read or write, had to beg a white guy, pretty obviously a student in my button-down shirt, chinos, and Converse All Stars. Though he repeated it several times, I couldn't understand or recognize the name of his birthplace, other than that it was somewhere in Georgia. We settled on Atlanta, because what the hell. I wrote that down, and I hope he got his card eventually, as I did.

Friends told me that Yale, presumptively prestigious to outside eyes, was known to insiders as "the armpit of the Ivy League." The other Ivies were in much nicer towns, some of them picturesque to the point of self-parody: Princeton, Cambridge, Philadelphia, Hanover, Providence, even boring upstate Ithaca, the farmer's Ivy with its notorious Suicide Gorge. All of them seemed preferable to a fractured blue-collar town on Long Island Sound whose best feature was its special style of coal-fired pizza. (Yes, it is excellent pizza.)

Social and financial distinctions are everywhere, in part because geography is everywhere, and geography is political. Risk, by the same token, is racial, cultural, and political, just like all status functions. Living as a white, extremely privileged four-year graduate student in a post-industrial northeastern American city that is about one-third each Black, Latino, and white taught me a lot of things, not all of them from books.

Officially, I was studying that branch of political philosophy known as justice theory—the question of basic social structure, justifiable schemes of distribution, fair procedures for dealing with the deficits of natural selection and risk. Unofficially, I was living in a kind of forever-unfolding, sometimes violent social experiment.

It was not Hobbes's state of nature, thankfully, but it was dangerous and illuminating in about equal measure.

Risk is *always* political. Let us now attempt to understand why and how that is the case, and—even more importantly—what might be done about it.

* * *

WHAT, THEN, ARE the specifically political dimensions of risk? In this section, I argue that there are three distinct orders of political risk, and that they are nested in ways that have been neglected by urban theory, traditional political theory, and public policy alike. Only by disentangling and then seeing the complex nesting of these risk-orders will we be able to appreciate the role that risk plays in geopolitical life. These political risks are geographical in a wide sense of that term: they are distributed and experienced over a terrain that blends topography with population, public policy with lived realities.

The most obvious order of risk is surely the consequences generated by at-risk populations around the globe. For numerous historical and political reasons, large chunks of the Earth's population face daily risks unknown to the rest of us. Food security, for example— the ability to count on regular and affordable supplies of daily sustenance—is a concern so far from the minds of most North Americans and Europeans that it can be extremely difficult even to imagine a half-hour of life in sub-Saharan Africa or parts of Asia. And yet there are large food deserts in many parts of these rich countries, where it is impossible to get fresh food, and one in nine Americans—forty million people—face various food security issues. We don't witness widespread famines in the United States or Canada, but instead have slow erosion of consistent access to affordable and healthy food for all citizens.

Potable water is an even more vivid example, since even the most privileged among the planet's seven billion human inhabitants now realize that a continued supply of fresh and non-toxic water is imperilled. The tainted-water scandals in Flint, Michigan, and Walkerton, Ontario, are timely, if also nasty, reminders of how fragile the global freshwater table is even in the developed world. Elsewhere, the scandal is a daily reality, including among many Indigenous communities in Canada. Physical risks of this sort pose associated dangers over supply and control. Violence is more prevalent in nations where resource scarcity is an ongoing, systemic problem.*

And so those persons who find themselves living under such conditions have traditionally felt that they have legitimate demands on those with the resources to alleviate actual and possible harms. This is the moral basis of claims for disaster relief, poverty and disease control, food security, and reduction of yawning wealth inequality. Let's call this cluster of issues *Order-One Risk*.

But there is already a hint of another dimension of risk in play here. The inhabitants of risky populations and areas did not choose their position; it is the result of a particularly nasty feature of what is known as the *birth-*

....

* See, for example, the work of Thomas Homer-Dixon, beginning with a landmark article called "Environmental Scarcities and Violent Conflict: Evidence from Cases," *International Security* 19:1 (1994): 5–40. This was later followed by both a general-audience overview in the *Atlantic* and a book, *Environment, Scarcity, and Violence* (Princeton, NJ: Princeton University Press, 2001).

right lottery. Where I am born, and who I am born to be, is a matter of luck, but it is luck of an especially far-reaching kind. Thus, further upstream of these urgent questions of relief and aid is another dimension of risk, concerning the distribution of risk itself. What are the politics here?

Most risks can be divided into the chosen and the unchosen. In contrast to other situations where choice is a factor in human affairs, when it comes to the basic situation of life—where and who I am—we tend to discount chosen risk and inflate unchosen risk. That is, we tend to minimize aid for, or even punish, those who suffer from the outcomes of risky choices, and help or at least consider helping those shouldering the burdens of unchosen risk. So, for example, we typically have little sympathy for a gambler or property speculator who went all in on some chancy bet and ended up losing. "Tough luck," we say, implying that the bad luck was, in effect, purchased by the speculator or gambler as a matter of conscious agency. The big wrinkle is that bad outcomes from risky choices often fall on those who made what they thought were safe bets: negotiating a mortgage, investing in an apparently solid company, purchasing an airline ticket in good faith. And then, when the chips were down, as in a floor or a pandemic, the big players get bailed out while the mere punters watch their lives go underwater. The former are considered "too big to fail." The latter simply … fail. Bye-bye, thanks for playing, loser.

It can seem as though the world is rigged not only for the house always to win but for some corporate whales at the tables to make dumb bets with other people's money and then simply walk away to cash out no matter what bad number came up. And, oh yeah, it can *seem* that way because it *is* that way. And attention is not paid to losers—just another insult-to-injury feature of the larger risk economy.

When risk is distributed both unevenly and without consent, we like to pretend that it is right to favour the unfavoured—even if we often, in practice, fail to follow through on that noble thought. Someone who had the no-fault misfortune of being born in a degraded environment with imminent prospects of struggle and violence is not usually simply labelled—unless those doing the labelling are ruthless to the point of cynicism—a mere case of tough luck. We call it, instead, misfortune. And misfortune is significant because we consider it to have some moral traction on us, something on the path to injustice. And yet, how often do we really follow through on these feelings, and how quickly do they fade? A sudden and highly publicized disaster will get attention and maybe some charitable relief. But distance makes selfish moral failures of us all. Meanwhile, systemic problems that are not distant are even less likely to be addressed, because they are made invisible within the overarching structure. It takes sustained effort to illuminate how certain kinds of apparent misfortunes are in fact injustices.

The gambler has no one to blame but himself, we say, unless we endorse social-influence or addiction theories of a far-reaching kind. But even the addiction narrative usually involves elements of choice and responsibility. If addiction is a monster like Homer Simpson's imagined, neon-clawed Gamblor, it is a metaphorical one, and thus a beast we believe can be slain through a combination of guidance, contextual support, and willpower. Hence the most sympathetic observer of someone taking bad risks by choice will likely insist that there is always a measure of personal responsibility in play, even in those cases where robust personal autonomy has been partially compromised. Gamblers are not automatons, and choice matters even when it is complicated.*

By contrast, when there is no matter of choice in play—where, in fact, there cannot be—even a grim observer will have a hard time maintaining that the risk incurred is a matter of personal responsibility. Central to this issue is not just the fact but the *supreme power* of the birthright lottery. The overarching fact of human existence is that we do not choose who and where we are born, nor do we choose most of the consequences of those facts. This lottery—captured by the notion of "tell me who your parents are and I will tell you who you are"—governs the bulk of life chances for all humans. Let's call this *Order-Two Risk*, since it generates many (or most) of the conditions considered in Order-One Risk.

Order-Two Risk can be spectral. What I mean is that smokescreens of various kinds work to conceal its political essence. For example, if you had the "good sense" to be born to wealthy parents in the developed world, your chances of comfort, long life, and happiness are maximized. You might even begin to think that this highly contingent outcome is something you engineered out of personal virtue. Thus the spectacle of Excessive Entitlement Disorder (sometimes also called "affluenza"), whereby a lucky sod is born on third base and grows up

....

* An excellent philosophical discussion of the nuances here can be found in Neil Levy, "Autonomy and Addiction," *Canadian Journal of Philosophy* 36:3 (2006): 427–47, especially 432 and 431.

thinking he hit a triple. Good luck is here comprehensively confused with virtue, skill, or intelligence.

As one writer noted about family wealth concentration, "Roughly 40 percent of all household wealth stems from inheritances. This means that 40 percent of why some Americans are extraordinarily well off has nothing to do with smarts, hard work, frugality, lucky gambles or entrepreneurial ingenuity. It is simply because they were born to rich parents."* The journalist did not use the word, but we might call this a particularly virulent economic form of *biofascism*, where family is assumed to be the dominant hub of social organization, despite what people (and laws) say about individuals or, sometimes, wider communities.

Hence the urgent need for more robust estate taxes as a simple matter of egalitarian correction, and to combat the insane degree of wealth inequality that exists in the United States and, to a lesser extent, in other wealthy Western countries. In the American case, the inequality is also significantly racialized, with white households twice as likely to receive an inheritance of any kind, and where median wealth of Black households is a scant 9 percent of that enjoyed in white households.

Neighbourhoods that are identified as historically Black have been destroyed to make way for freeways; other neighbourhoods are created explicitly to exclude Black people or Latinos. Loans are denied to people of colour for specious and arbitrary, but actually highly motivated, rea-

....

* Lily Batchelder, "Tax the Rich and Their Heirs: How to Tax Inheritances More Fairly," *New York Times*, June 24, 2020. Batchelder, a law professor, notes that baby boomers and the generation that came before them "currently own $84-trillion, or 81 percent of all U.S. household wealth."

sons. Some subdivisions, including the utopian suburban Levittown developments in New York, New Jersey, and Maryland, included deed regulations backed by the Federal Housing Association to exclude Black owners. Voting districts are redrawn into bizarre shapes and gerrymandered in order to prevent any preponderance of voters—you know who they are, we all know who they are—who might upset the current arrangement.* And when in doubt, simply turn a citizen away at the polling place for another specious or arbitrary reason. This is racial prejudice hardened into law and public policy.

Most taxation schemes, even the ones that have some semblance of fairness in graduated levels, create fortress-like bulwarks of wealth and privilege against justice. They create client citizens who begin to consider community as a contract of dollars for services, rather than a shared undertaking with a gift economy at its centre. The canard that estate or inheritance tax is double-dipping, for example—a tax upon wealth already taxed in its acquisition—is the result of wilful conceptual stupidity, and complicity with unexamined ideas about family, comfort, and self-protection. What is taxed on an estate or an inheritance is the *transfer* of wealth, not the notional nest egg itself. Inherited wealth should be taxed at higher rates than income from work or investment, not lower. (I will have more to say about taxes in the next section.)

....

* Three Chicago-based graphic designers created an entire font of letterforms made up of contorted American Congressional districts whose boundaries were redrawn to prevent the influence of "undesirable" voters. See Kayla Epstein, "How Do You Spell 'Gerrymandering Is Bad?' with a Font Made out of Preposterous Districts," *Washington Post*, August 2, 2019. The font sports the excellent name "Ugly Gerry."

That baseball-derived metaphor about third base and triples was often used to describe former US president George W. Bush, surely anyone's idea of a beneficiary of family wealth and influence—though, as often noted in 2020, not nearly as bad in Trump-tinted retrospect as many critics suggested. This mediocre scion of a powerful family attended Yale University as a "legacy" applicant. This is itself a traditional practice of preference that functions as a sort of frequent-flyer program for the wealthy who convert their cash, in the form of reliable donations, into cachet, in the form of an Ivy League degree (I won't say education). But more than this, Bush entered the White House as president of the United States, despite being drastically underqualified, because of a network of influence that, in another context, would have landed him a comfortable chair on the New York Stock Exchange. Indeed, from the point of view of the Bush family circle, the two offices are more or less the same thing.

Such influence peddling is offensive all by itself, but is made exponentially worse by the delusion that the resulting success was somehow earned rather than granted. There is no virtue in being born to rich parents, any more than there is vice in being born to poor ones. But these obvious facts can be hard to see through the mists of delusion that settle around wealth and power. This is the essence of Randian entitlement, that bizarre stew of anti-collectivism and aggressive individualism that suffuses the tortuous novels of Ayn Rand. Here, in *The Fountainhead* (1943) or *Atlas Shrugged* (1957), all success is purely the result of individual creativity and effort, parasitically drained by the forces of altruism, taxation, and the general good. Never mind that, in fact, there is no such success without markets, and workers, and the infrastructure that makes economies possible—not least the baseline existence of money, that collective fantasy-token of trust and co-operation.

More recently, the same phenomenon of transmuting inherited wealth into personal virtue can be observed in Donald Trump. During the 2016 presidential electoral campaign, the unlikely and ill-qualified Republican presidential candidate liked to portray himself as a self-made man, even a man of the people, conveniently obliterating the fact that his worldly success was made possible by a hefty inheritance and a history of shady dealing bordering on malfeasance or fraud. The *New Yorker* satirist Andy Borowitz nailed the point with an imagined news article headlined "Trump Economic Plan Calls for Every American to Inherit Millions from Father." According to the article, Trump made a rallying speech about the economy: "'There are people at my rallies, desperate people, desperate because they want jobs,' he told his luncheon audience at the Detroit Economic Club. 'Once they inherit millions from their father, they will never want a job again.'"*

* * *

SUCH EXTREME CASES are targets of easy satire—although, as the succeeding years of the first Trump administration demonstrate, a person impervious to self-knowledge is capable of weathering not only sustained satire but the very advent of truth and factual criticism, a person capable indeed of rewriting history on a daily basis via a

* Andy Borowitz, "Trump Economic Plan Calls for Every American to Inherit Millions from Father," *New Yorker*, August 8, 2016.

Twitter feed, a revolving-door policy on disloyal (that is, independently minded and responsible) advisers, and bullying press briefings. But political theorists have struggled with birthright lottery, in large measure because its contingencies seem so intractable. How could one ever hope to stem the tide of consequences brought about by the brute facts of birth and situation? Every *post facto* justice measure would be climbing uphill against the steep grade of chance. And are we perhaps overstepping the bounds of legitimate intervention if we try to advance such measures? Perhaps there are simply some things that remain misfortunes rather than injustices?

Any conceivable distinction between misfortune and injustice is open to criticism. Is the New Orleans flood, say, merely an act of God (misfortune) or a matter of heinously bad infrastructure (injustice)? When does inept government count more than the simple bad luck of living in a drowned parish? Taking a necessary broader view, what does the institution of Black slavery or the colonization of Indigenous people do to future life chances of generations that follow decades, even centuries, later?

To answer these thorny questions, many people follow the lead of John Rawls's foundational work on justice as fairness, and have adopted versions of his idea of the "original position." This is an imagined-choice scenario in which the specific circumstances of birth are excluded by a "veil of ignorance," thus freeing choosers to settle on schemes of justification and basic social structure that are fair to all.* Note that, when we imagine what rules of the social game we might choose if we didn't know who our

---

* John Rawls, *A Theory of Justice* (Cambridge, MA: Belknap Press, 1970). My characterization is spare but I hope not inaccurate.

parents (or our postal code) might be, the basic lottery is assumed. The uneven natural distribution of favours is what makes justice an issue in the first place.

Some critics have balked at the idea of such ignorance-based choice as the basis of legitimate social policy, but consider for a moment the core insight. If I don't know who, in particular, I am, then I really do have a basic rational stake in upholding practices of fairness in distributing goods and life chances. A simple analogy captures the point. Suppose I am asked by my mother to cut the remaining portion of a pie into two sections, one for me and one for my brother. The catch is that, while I *cut* first, he gets to *choose* first. The only rational action on my part is to opt for equal shares of the remaining pie. Any other course is self-defeating, given an assumption of basic rationality on the part of my brother (he will choose the larger piece, given the chance). The original position in effect models a complex version of this scenario: we all can do the cutting, but nobody knows who is going to get to do the choosing.

Here I want to postulate yet another order of risk. It brings together the luck of the lottery with the original-choice model's notion of consenting participants, but with a new twist. This *Order-Three Risk* concerns the relative levels of *aversion* and *tolerance* regarding risk itself, qualities that might themselves be distributed unevenly within a population. Indeed, all evidence shows that the distribution of tolerance to risk is wildly uneven. Some people are simply more inclined to take chances—to shoulder risk—than others. Moreover, they consider this risky behaviour rational, by their own internal lights. They don't simply like bungee jumping or roller coasters, they consider them a safe and fun way to pass the time. Part of the fun is the assumed or implied risk, always backed by a belief that nothing bad will happen—to them, this time, right now. (Because bad things do happen to bungee jumpers and roller coaster riders.*)

This variance in risk tolerance is neither a matter of brute injustice in circumstances nor entirely a function of the (closely related) chances of who our parents are— though we have to allow for the effects of a secure environment on cultivating risk tolerance. If I know I am going to be bailed out if I get arrested, or given a new job if I blow my current one, risks are a lot easier to take. Nature meets nurture in risk, as it does so often in life generally. In other words, Order-Three Risk can be seen as distinct from both Order-One and Order-Two Risk, even as it blends with them, because it concerns individual orientation to risk in general. It is an independent personal relationship to chance that can, under certain circumstances, govern significant outcomes for other people.

How so? Well, imagine, once again, that we are in an original-choice position such as Rawls's thought experiment. Some people might opt for unequal outcomes, on the chance that they would enjoy the fruits of inequality. They gamble on the benefits of unfair distribution working in their favour.

In this way, risk-tolerant participants in the choice game can skew results in favour of social rules that allow steep inequalities, with no welfare floor. These players may

....

* Philosophers and psychologists have taken to calling this combination of believing one is (mostly) safe, even while entertaining countervailing feelings of danger or fear, a condition of *alief*, as distinct from straightforward belief. The term was coined by philosopher Tamar Szabó Gendler in "Alief and Belief," *Journal of Philosophy* 105:10 (2008): 634–63.

lose their gamble; but meanwhile *everybody* loses because the game is skewed against fairness. And this is exactly what obtains in the so-called real world. Neo-liberal economics dominates life and choice, favouring the favoured while maintaining a narrative of *possible* success for others—the American Dream or some similar bill of goods.

Once more, we could solve this problem by theoretically ruling aversion and tolerance out of the ideal situation. Attitude to risk (we might argue), in common with other personal factors such as height or physical beauty, must be excluded from one's self-knowledge under the conditions of ideal choice. This will clear the way for rational agreement about society's basic structure.

But this move looks merely ad hoc, and therefore unjustified. More significantly, these behind-the-veil risk-positive people are just idealized cousins to the free market risk-takers of the actual world, those who believe that they deserve larger outcomes because of what they have ventured. Such people don't believe they were born on third base; they believe they took a chance on a hanging off-speed pitch and hustled their way to that triple.

We can better understand the significance of Order-Three Risk by bringing it into even closer relation to the other two orders of risk. If risk aversion and risk tolerance themselves become part of the birthright lottery, and not pure personal virtues, then the game changes decisively. Cheerleaders for "entrepreneurship" and "innovation" love to argue that risk tolerance is an admirable, cultivated quality, like courage or temperance (even if often ventured with other people's money). But what if it is more of an inherited tendency and, as such, a morally vacuous feature, like height or beauty? This "essential" quality of self might be just as much a matter of who your parents are as whether you were born in happy Denmark or afflicted sub-Saharan Africa.

Consider, here, the relationship long observed historically between theodicy and geography. Perhaps the most celebrated defence of theodicy is that of Gottfried Wilhelm Leibniz—he coined the term in a 1710 treatise. The notion was challenged savagely by Voltaire after the 1755 Lisbon earthquake, which killed as many as fifty thousand people and destroyed 85 percent of that city. In his "Poem on the Lisbon Disaster" (1756) and especially, as mentioned before, in the 1759 satire *Candide*, Voltaire mocked the doctrine of a benevolent deity creating the best of all possible worlds, making it instead into a kind of violent disaster movie. (The book's quietist conclusion, "We must tend our own gardens," was not in fact Voltaire's way. A critic of dogmatism to the last, he was denied a Christian burial but was secretly interred at the Abbey of Scellières in Champagne, where a relative was the abbot. His heart and brain were embalmed separately, which I for one consider awesome.)

Many thinkers about risk have since noted its geographical features, which are often quite strange. Humans choose to live in areas that are known to be risky, for reasons that range from familial or clan attachment to inertia and scientifically irrational beliefs in divine presence. But as geographical risk specialist Iain Stewart has argued, "hazards emerge from nature, disasters are made in society."[*] In other words, hazard is a morally and politically

....

* Ben Major, "Un-natural Hazards: The Cultural Geography of Risk," *Summary of Keynote Address*, Professor Iain Stewart, Geographical Association Annual Conference (2009).

neutral fact, like the weather; a hazard becomes a disaster only when humans and their property are involved. The linking term, which combines a logic of natural events with a logic of human apprehension, is of course *risk*. As Stewart argues, "hazards are predictable and recurring events, often returning to the same region, and yet knowledge of this fact does not stop people from continuing to rebuild in the same place."[*] Why is this so?

One large reason is that even geographically localized risk is not experienced in an equitable way. One can think of adjoining neighbourhoods where risk levels rise or fall dramatically—this is a too-common feature of many American cities—but here we note cases where the very same geographical location can support different levels of risk tolerance precisely because the people living there are differently situated in other ways. "Indeed," Stewart notes, "it is often the wealthy that choose to live in physically hazardous settings, convinced that it is safe to build palatial homes on hurricane-prone shores, perched precariously on steep unstable slopes or amidst incendiary scrub."[†] The implied references should be obvious: the disproportionate number of poor and Black residents of New Orleans after Hurricane Katrina in 2005; the ability of richer Californians to save their homes during the wildfires of 2019. These are features of the cultural geography of risk—which is also, and always, a socio-economic geography.

The wealthy take these chances, Stewart concludes, "because their affluence can buy superior engineering, which affords some degree of protection, but more because

....

* Ibid.

† Ibid.

the social and economic resilience of the owners offsets their acute physical vulnerability."* Your house was destroyed by flood or fire? Buy a new one somewhere else! Your clothes and furniture are ruined by water damage? Replace them! These forms of structural injustice, whereby some otherwise risky choices are made less risky because of prior wealth, in turn create other injustice markets, in the form of status luxury goods. My ability to afford the risk-recovery strategies of easily getting new shelter and clothing is made to seem an enviable trait, or good luck, even if that trait is one that I did nothing to earn or deserve.

Humans in general underrate risk and overrate resiliency. The richer among us can afford that meta-bet on risky behaviour; most of us cannot, yet somehow believe we can. Indeed, new evidence suggests that risk maps—which direct home-buying decisions as well as assistance relief from federal programs—are skewed against marginalized neighbourhoods, often those that are also for similar reasons racialized. As one American commentator notes, "In two-thirds of states, minority neighborhoods shoulder more undisclosed flood risk than the state average. That gap could have significant ramifications for citizens in those areas to access finance, including mortgages, property insurance, and post-disaster recovery funds."† This is the geography of risk rendered into graphic form.

This combination of facts and fears in turn suggests that the distribution of attitude to risk—Order-Three Risk—demands corrective justice considerations. That is in large part because a risk-tolerant attitude is now under-

....

* Ibid.

† Tim McDonnell, "How New Flood Maps Could Undermine Marginalized Neighborhoods," *Quartz*, July 5, 2020.

stood as a function of socio-economic status, a species of luxury good, not a natural trait like left-handedness or even adventitious physical beauty. The more money I have, the more security I can purchase; the more security I can purchase, the more risk I can tolerate. Even insurance schemes, which as we saw previously are intended to share and offset risk, are a product of privilege: to be able to afford insurance is itself a sign of status, not a measure of one's personal risk aversion or risk tolerance.

Thus we might need to control for, rather than merely assume, the uneven distributions of willingness to take chances. Indeed, if such distributions are having negative systemic effects at the widest level, reinforcing schemes of governance that favour risk tolerance, we should view regulation of Order-Three Risk as a central tenet of any just society. We can tolerate marginal gains scored by those who are physically attractive or athletically blessed (Gisele Bündchen and Tom Brady are simply going to be better off than most people, given the world as we find it), but we would certainly not want such features to govern general outcomes of life chances for everyone. Risk tolerance might be just as adventitious, and so just as irrelevant.

The political conclusion becomes ever more obvious: risk is a matter for justice interventions at all conceptual levels. Loosening the sense of "deserved" connection between personal qualities such as risk tolerance and good outcomes is just as important as alleviating the consequences of Order-One Risk. Without both aspects, any attempt to realize justice concerning the consequences of birthright lottery will be hampered. Such attempts will fail to address the ongoing sense among the favoured that they—and hence others—have what they have by right, and so those less favoured likewise deserve the poor outcomes that are generated by the current arrangement.

In one clear and traditional sense, justice means to favour the *un*favoured, giving aid where it is called for. But perhaps to be more complete, justice also demands that we unfavour the favoured. The core lesson is actually an old and familiar one, with new and renewed urgency. When it comes to the politics of risk, it is not enough to comfort the afflicted; we must also afflict the comfortable. This may involve, as a first step, thinking of people not merely as isolated individuals, self-contained bundles of rights and responsibilities, but as members of historically disadvantaged groups or targeted subpopulations with special claims beyond their formal legal status.* It will also involve some sharp criticism of other formalistic fallacies, such as equality before the law, or the claim that one person gets just one vote.

When the 2010 Citizens United decision of the American Supreme Court recognized corporate campaign spending as a form of protected political speech, it merely enshrined in law what everyone has always known: money does indeed talk.† But what everyone has always known

....

* An essential text is Will Kymlicka, *Liberalism, Community, and Culture* (Oxford: Clarendon Press, 1989), which the philosopher has expanded and elaborated in later volumes. He is also a passionate advocate of non-human animal rights, which I do not have space to address here but which are well worth considering in terms of larger political demands, as indeed are the rights of potential non-human artificial beings. The latter is something I have been addressing recently in lectures and articles, the subject of a future book from McGill-Queen's University Press. Meanwhile, and with apologies for citing my own stuff again, there's this: "Are Sentient AIs Persons?" in Markus D. Dubber, Frank Pasquale, and Sunit Das, eds., *The Oxford Handbook of Ethics of AI* (New York: Oxford University Press, 2020), pp. 325-42.

† Citizens United v. Federal Election Commission, 588 U. S. 310 (2010).

can be changed, or at least countered. The world is altering rapidly, indeed every day, under pandemic conditions. There are clawbacks and retrenchments of various kinds, the rush to return to dark dreams of Fortress Normal. There are also, thank the gods of luck and human effort, new efforts at reform and moral accounting.

This is one of those times where you have to choose a side. And to do that, you had better know, as well as you can, the odds governing your bet.

4. Death and Taxes

THE HORIZON OF all risk is death. As we know, or should, this ultimate numbers game conforms to the classic pigeonhole principle mentioned earlier in the discussion of the birthday problem.*

What is that principle? When many slots are filled via population density over probable events, the certitude of an outcome grows closer and closer to 100 percent. Probability gets very high indeed with many pigeons for many holes; and when all holes are filled, all bets are off because there is no gap between pigeons and holes. And we are the pigeons. We all die, and nothing can forestall or alter that final wager of life. We may choose to believe otherwise, or wager unreasonably when jumping out of airplanes or heading into combat, but the snake eyes always come up eventually, like it or not.

Mostly, we don't like it; hence the ever-renewing versions of warding off and bargaining. We are forcibly

....

* See note p 84.

reminded here that Elisabeth Kübler-Ross's five-stage model of grief includes bargaining as the *third* stage—after anger and denial, before depression and eventual acceptance—and hence, we might say, is the crux of the model, its rational-irrational fulcrum.* I want to negotiate! But there is no bargaining with mortality, and any bet here is, ultimately, a sucker's bet. The house always wins, because the house is the universe itself.

That includes any notion of the universe as a multiverse: possible worlds in which I may live longer, given different life choices, cannot reasonably preclude the bottom-line judgment of death itself. If they did, such worlds would not be ones we could recognize as inhabitable. As Martin Heidegger and other existential philosophers have long reminded us, death is our most proximate and "ownmost" possibility: which is to say, death is the work that cannot be outsourced, that must be executed by each of us, alone at the end. You cannot delegate existential tasks.

Philosophers of another kind have likewise long sought to reassure us that death is not something to fear. Ever since Socrates declared it not an event experienced in life, in Plato's *Phaedo*, other strong-minded thinkers have worked to convince themselves, and us, of similar propositions. Wittgenstein noted in his *Tractatus Logico-Philosophicus* (1921) that "[d]eath is not an event in life: we do not live to experience death. If we take eternity to mean not infinite temporal duration but timelessness, then eternal life belongs to those who live in the present."†

....

* Elisabeth Kübler-Ross, *On Death and Dying* (London: Routledge, 1969); see also my favourite book about death and the fear thereof (yes, I know, don't ask) Julian Barnes, *Nothing to Be Frightened Of* (New York: Knopf, 2008).

† Ludwig Wittgenstein, *Tractatus Logico-Philosophicus*, Proposition 6.4311.

Sure! And, for the record, I wouldn't mind having "Eternal life belongs to those who live in the present" inscribed on my headstone. But does it help, really, with the bets of life as we live them? Derek Parfit, the dean of analytic philosophers in the English tradition, wrote this after achieving a rational rejection of presumptive personal identity over time: "After my death, there will be no one living who will be me," he argued. "My death will break the more direct relations between my present experiences and future experiences, but it will not break various other relations." He concluded this way: "Now that I have seen this, my death seems to me less bad."*

Well, sure again. But Derek Parfit is still dead, as of January 2017, and that matters a lot to many of us even if, per logical necessity, it cannot matter to him.

Philosophers are divided over method when it comes to death. Some would have us dwell in and explore our anxiety about death. Others would have us acknowledge that there is no good reason for this anxiety in the first place. Both classes of thinker are united in a desire for us to accept and accommodate our finitude, the final risk event whose probabilities are always 100 percent. Does it help to dwell, or to deny? Perhaps. But my sense, as a philosopher, is that death will not be quelled. Socrates speculated that all of philosophy was a matter of learning how to die. Yes, indeed: *how*, but not *whether*, *why*, or *when*. Those categories are beyond all reason, and all specific or actuarial calculations of risk. And as for *who*—well, we all know for whom the bell tolls, sooner or later.

....

* Parfit, *Reasons and Persons*, 281–82.

So, yes, we will all expire. But while we are here, we have opportunities, costs and benefits, and above all the ability to *think*. We can consider our mortality, perhaps alone among the creatures we know, and we can choose to live safely and well, and create a world that cannot ever eliminate risk but can distribute it more justly.

Individual, unalterable death is the horizon of my existence. This is a fact. It matters very little in any cosmic sense whether I live or die. This is likewise a fact. Most of us are destined to be forgotten, usually sooner rather than later. Fact again. Achilles may have fought for glory and eternal memory, but for every Achilles there is an Ozymandias who, as Shelley's much-quoted sonnet (1818) reminds us, is remembered only because forgotten:

And on the pedestal, these words appear:
"My name is Ozymandias, King of Kings;
Look on my Works, ye Mighty, and despair!"
Nothing beside remains. Round the decay
Of that colossal Wreck, boundless and bare
The lone and level sands stretch far away.

There is no eternity so immeasurable that it cannot erase the memories of even the most celebrated from among our number.

When it comes to the risk of death—taxes we will discuss in a moment—there really is literally nothing to be done and very little even to consider. You roll the dice and you take your chances. The peculiar fact that you were not privy to the decision (really happenstance) that brought you into this existential casino in the first instance is just part of how the game, and the town, is rigged. People love to say what happens in Vegas stays in Vegas! This sentiment is considered liberatory, a get-out-of-moral-jail-free card for the *Hangover* movie franchise or every bad-idea bachelor's trip and couples weekend caper. A better cinematic trope, to my mind, is the spectacle of Jon Favreau and Vince Vaughn as struggling Los Angeles acting wannabes setting out for the desert in search of fortune and fun in *Swingers* (1996). "Vegas, baby, Vegas!" they shout to each other. "You're so money!" Then reality sets in: a double-down blackjack bet scoops their wallets of three hundred dollars and leaves them high and dry just a few scant minutes into purported adventure. Their slick suits and painted 1940s ties still look good ...

So, okay, whatever. Like many people, I've been to Las Vegas, or "Lost Wages" as my father used to call it, a tired old joke. Even in its late-model New Strip glory, with leading acts on mainstages and restaurants sanctioned by world-class chefs, I found it tawdry and frankly depressing, a glitzy palace of broken dreams linked by endless streams of sweaty people in cargo shorts and tank tops plus a maze of confusing underground passageways. I confess I did enjoy the rainbow-hued alcohol-freezie drinks to be had every dozen yards on the sidewalks of the Strip. But all this staged-and-celebrated liberation is, even at the best of times—when you come up a winner—a voucher, not a pass. What happens here does not, in fact, stay here.

I won on the slot machines at Caesars Palace in Vegas—yay!—and went over to change my ticket for cash, about twelve dollars and fifty cents. I admired the total seriousness with which the cashier passed over my winnings. This was happily reminiscent of two other very tiny gambling strokes of success I have enjoyed in a mostly non-betting life.

One of these came playing blackjack at a laid-back casino in Antigua. It was nothing like those high-stakes games of all-in poker in the James Bond Bahamas, where voluptuous women ride horses on the beach, every car in the lot is a million-dollar sweetheart, and you can order champagne and caviar to your villa from room service. In Antigua, the dealers were funny, the cigars and rum punch were cheap, and I scored US$150 by souring my uncle's cards as he sat next to me, one card down the table. He kept complaining I was taking his cards, hitting on fifteens and doing other dumb things. But somehow I came out on top, and was later handed a fistful of the American dollars so prized in the Caribbean.

So yes, I suppose I have been, now and then, a briefly favoured swain of Lady Luck—what the pulp magazines used to call *just a lucky guy* or *a lucky stiff*, an Average Joe who sometimes rolled right, not ever a real player. (The *stiff* in *lucky stiff* implies that you're undeserving, lacking in skill or wits, just as fortunate whether alive or dead.)

I was certainly luckier, anyway, than Peter Lorre's character Signor Ugarte in *Casablanca* (1942), cashing in his chips even as the police close in, guns blazing. The buildup to this famous scene in a film full of them, where Humphrey Bogart's Rick Blaine "sticks his neck out for nobody," contains two explicit mentions of luck, both of them ominous in their different ways.

Ugarte tells Rick he has two letters of transit, "signed by Général de Gaulle himself" which "cannot be rescinded, not even questioned." These letters are the film's Hitchcockian MacGuffin, albeit anachronistically so: the still centre of the narrative action, the obscure object of desire, the token of freedom that everyone wants. They are the ultimate casino chips of life and death. Ugarte has, we are made to see, murdered the German couriers who were in possession of them, to sell later for a profit.

"Too bad about those two German couriers, wasn't it?" Ugarte says to the apparently bored Rick. The latter says, cynically: "They got a lucky break. Yesterday they were just two German clerks. Today they're the 'honoured dead.'" Ugarte, who trusts Rick precisely because he despises the chintzy peddler, gives the saloon keeper the letters for safekeeping. "Rick, I hope you're more impressed with me now," Ugarte says. "Now if you'll excuse me, I'll share my luck with your roulette table." This is Free French territory, so the roulette wheel doesn't feature the notorious double-zero slot that kills any gambler's fighting chance. Doesn't matter: Ugarte can only win for losing. He gets arrested soon after his run of luck at the wheel, the frantic gunshots, and Rick's refusal to hide him. The next day he is shot while trying to escape—or was it suicide? Captain Renault has not quite decided ...

High roller or low, deadbeat or whale, you never get out of the big jail. What happens on the mortal plane stays there too—because where else could you ever go? The house always wins, sure, but you have no choice except to play. But you also have the choice to play *well*, like wearing a mask, washing your hands, and not going to some crowded bar or hyped political rally when all available factual evidence suggests that these are just smart things to do. Indeed, you have the choice to be smart rather than dumb, though always within our feeble human limits. You can bet on a new normal of a more just world rather than a too-hasty return to the same old walled-in city.

Perhaps, then, the wisdom of all these disparate philosophers becomes oddly conjoined. Remain vigilant about your mortality, as the existentialists enjoin, and feel the heavy weight of responsibility that comes with that; but likewise embrace the lightness of Parfit's self-emancipation from the "glass tunnel" of taking your specific personal identity too seriously. You are here, and you will someday be gone. That is enough, because it must be enough. As Ethel Barrymore would say, that's all there is, there isn't any more.

* * *

MY DEATH IS merely one very small data point in the network of inevitable demise. It matters a lot to me, sure, yet almost certainly not very much to the world, or multiverse, at large. But let's consider two higher degrees of potential death: the extinction of *many*, and the extinction of *all*. A pandemic is, depending on your proclivities, a disaster or a time-limited breach in the normal. But when does the latter fold into the former? How many have to die before something counts as truly disastrous? How many people have to die a certain way, or in a certain place, or of a certain race?

The extinction of many is a ready subject for study, because it involves everything we know, or think we know, about risk. But it has rarely been pursued with its political implications in mind. *Many*, for our current purposes, might range from several humans (a family killed in a car crash, say, or by visitation from a serial killer—obviously two vastly different probabilities) to dozens, hundreds, or even thousands of humans felled at one stroke.

We have seen already that *disasters*—which is to say, human suffering and tragedy as a result of natural hazard—are both common and commonly ignored. The news cycle is short and relentless, the capacity of people to exercise empathetic concern very quickly eroded by multiple demands, new distractions, and the inevitable compassion fatigue that comes with living on a planet with close to eight billion other people. None of us matters that much. Life is cheap here in Casino Earth. The cultural and economic reasons for these forms of ignorance and distraction are politically significant and a direct prompt on extensions of our basic thinking about justice. Okay, good to know—and perhaps to act upon, if we are up to the challenge. But what about human hazards causing human disasters, and our attendant unwillingness to admit error? An important degree up from my death is the act, or series of them, that leads to the death of many—and this too, with bells on, is a justice issue. Can these be prevented, and if so, how exactly? Risk is social in more than one fashion, as we now have cause to see in our complicated, interconnected world.

Here's a classic case in point. On July 7, 2017, near midnight, Air Canada flight 759, with 135 passengers and five crew aboard, crashed into four taxiing passenger aircraft at San Francisco International Airport after missing its assigned runway. More than a thousand people were killed or injured, and the dreaded cause following investigation—pilot error—showed that the Air Canada captain was overtired because of the Canadian carrier's industry-substandard rest restrictions and misheard the control tower's instructions. New regulations were put in place, but nothing could restore the lost lives and livelihoods that resulted from the crash.

The nice thing about this story is that it didn't happen that way. AC759 was able to avert the crash when one of the pilots awaiting takeoff notified the tower of the aberrant flight path and another, commanding a Philippine Airlines ship, turned on his landing lights as a warning. The Air Canada captain abruptly changed course, flew low over the planes on the ground, and later landed safely. This so-called near miss—actually better described as a near crash—does not appear on the statistics about air safety, and yet it has been much studied precisely because it illustrates the omnipresence of risks averted. There but for the grace of something intangible goes a crashing airplane.[*]

Non-events are metaphysically distinct from actual events in obvious ways; and yet they sketch the contours of human life on every level, from the minor trip on a loose stair that did not lead to a broken neck to the city-wide disaster that was averted because of early warning and calm evacuation. Death at scales small and large is the ever-present fact of existence. Safety measures and protocols are the social equivalents of insurance schemes: using statistics from past events, we try to articulate standards and procedures that will lessen, even if never entirely eliminate, the risks of living together with others. But statistics usually gathers num-

[*] Linda Besner, "Once in a Blue Moon: What We Can Learn from Things That Never Happened," *Globe and Mail*, August 9, 2019.

bers about things that happened. What about all the other things that didn't happen but might have—a far, far larger set of possible data?

There are, naturally, entire statistical subdisciplines dedicated to understanding all manner of non-events and near misses. But here statistical analysis, elsewhere marshalled as the governing fact set of actuarial study, sometimes begins to resemble theology rather than science. Hypotheses are many, conclusions are few, and evidence always contingent. Famous examples, including the Air Canada non-disaster, become famous. What we do know is that systems are good when it comes to averting expected but always partly unknowable risks.

Another well-known aviation instance was the attempt, during the Second World War, to account for the flak damage on returning bomber and fighter planes. The aircraft showed heavy damage on the wings and control panels, prompting engineers to propose greater armour plating in these apparently vulnerable areas. That is, until someone realized that the significant planes were the ones *not* returning, which had presumably sustained structural fuselage damage. These, and not the near misses before them, were the statistically significant sample.

Veteran American reporter James Fallows, an amateur pilot, put it this way in a long essay about the United States' failed response to the coronavirus pandemic during the summer of 2020: "Controlling the risks of flight may not be as complex as fighting a pandemic, but it's in the ballpark. Aviation is fundamentally a very dangerous activity. People are moving at high altitudes, at high speed, and in high volume, with a guarantee of mass casualties if things go wrong. Managing the aviation system involves hardware—airframes, engines, flight control systems—and 'software,' in the form of training, routing, and coordinated protocols."

And so: "It requires recognition of hazards that are certain—bad weather, inevitable mechanical breakdowns—and those that cannot be specifically foreseen, from terrorist episodes to obscure but consequential computer bugs." And therefore finally: "It involves businesses and also governments; it is nation-specific and also worldwide; it demands second-by-second attention and also awareness of trends that will take years to develop."[*]

These are exactly the conditions and failures that make for disaster when the hazards happen and responses do not. "Aviation is safe in large part because it learns from its disasters," Fallows argued. Nobody wants the disasters, or even near disasters; everybody benefits from the learning.

Fallows: "The modern aviation system works. From the dawn of commercial aviation through the 1990s, 1,000 to 2,000 people would typically die each year in airline crashes. Today, the worldwide total is usually about one-tenth that level. Last year, before the pandemic began, more than 25,000 commercial-airline flights took off each day from airports in the United States. Every one of them landed safely."

And so then consider a thought experiment whose results will shock nobody: "What if the NTSB were brought in to look at the Trump administration's handling of the pandemic? What would its investigation conclude? I'll jump to the answer before laying out the background: This was a journey straight into a mountainside, with countless

* James Fallows, "The Three Weeks That Changed Everything," *Atlantic*, June 29, 2020.

missed opportunities to turn away. A system was in place to save lives and contain disaster. The people in charge of the system could not be bothered to avoid the doomed course."[*]

Cases and situations of this disastrous and near-miss kind can be multiplied, in everything from engineering to industrial safety to politics. The Process Improvement Institute, for instance, estimates that for every workplace accident there are as many as one hundred potential ones that *almost happened but didn't.* If the non-event has statistical probability zero and the actual event statistical probability one, then near misses should probably (!) be assigned a value of 0.9 to encompass their massive but factually unrealized power.

Political scientists have likewise studied near misses in *democratic* collapse—a topic that cannot be far from mind in these days we are currently experiencing. They found that independent agencies and actors, judges and civil servants for example, including military forces and politicians, were far more effective in saving democracies from collapse than popular demonstrations or even uprisings. Analyzing Finland between the two world wars, Colombia in 2010, and Sri Lanka in 2015, researchers Tom Ginsburg and Aziz Huq did not discount popular dissent—it had both direct and indirect effects on social change—but concluded that office-holders and institutions were far more reliable curbs on autocracy.[†]

* * *

....

[*] Ibid.

[†] Tom Ginsburg and Aziz Huq, "Democracy's 'Near Misses,'" *Journal of Democracy* 29:4 (October 2018).

MY DEATH, THE death of many, possible and actual. We know—I realize I keep repeating this!—that the statistical probability of our own death is 1.0. But not at every given instant, only in the short-long mortal run. Every day I may avoid death, or cheat it as we sometimes say, dangerously. A dozen or a hundred small contingencies keep me here a little bit longer, as do another dozen or hundred others at the level of travel, urban life, shared spaces and air, daily transactions, and on and on. Here at this second level, whether we are talking flight safety or democracy, the probability of death can never be 1.0, even if it hovers around 0.9—or so we like to think.

Apologies to those seeking reassurance and comfort, but there is at least a third level of death to consider before we can consider our risk work done. I mean the probability of a so-called *extinction event*, or apocalypse.

Many years ago—and I thank the very same intangible laws of contingency for *how* many years ago, given all my unremarkable daily risks since then—I wrote a book about apocalyptic thinking.* It was a few years before the year 2000, and the looming millennial turning point seemed to prompt yet another in a well-documented series of cultural upheavals generated by anxiety. Exploring the history of millennial dread, I encountered the familiar calendar of events and dates: 1000, 1666, 1900; plagues, witches, fires, and fascism. It was all there, and the mid-1990s seemed not very much different: UFO fears, death cults, environmental degradation, and the like. The world survived the transition; even the much-touted computer bug that was supposed to crash the

* Mark Kingwell, *Dreams of Millennium: Report from a Culture on the Brink* (Toronto: Viking, 1996; New York: Faber and Faber, 1997).

world's digital systems failed to materialize. We all lurched into the year 2000—or 2001 if you're a math purist or Stanley Kubrick fan—with nothing much but a bit of ruffled cultural hair.

One article that caught my eye in all the reading about anxiety and dread was a sober disquisition by Martin H. Krieger called "Could the Probability of Doom Be Zero or One?" It appeared in the venerable *Journal of Philosophy* and discussed, among other things, the Kolmogorov zero-or-one law of probability theory—itself a matter of dispute, given something often designated as a law.[*] Kolmogorov's law has been criticized for not allowing intermediate probabilities such as the ones just discussed with respect to non-events. It also has the maybe-disturbing implication that doom events may definitely have either zero or one probability but (as the Wikipedia editors dryly put it) it is "surprisingly hard to determine which of these two extreme values is the correct one."[†]

The following quotation from Krieger gets everything right, and also in the right order: "Let us take doom to be the end of all possibilities. Doom has no consequents, in that there are no future choices." On doom's scope: "Whether that termination is my personal doom, my community's, or the earth's is open to question. But for our purposes, the crucial feature is that with doom there is no future, at least if the future is construed in terms of the kind of choices that lead up to doom." Thus: "In effect, doom is a limit or an endpoint of a series of actions (a path to doom)." Even accepting intermediate probabil-

....

[*] Martin H. Krieger, "Could the Probability of Doom Be Zero or One?" *Journal of Philosophy* 92:7 (July 1995): 382–87; quotations from p. 382.

[†] Drawn from the Wikipedia entry on Kolmogorov's Zero-or-One Law.

ities on particular events, a sequence of them can lead to a looming probability of one. "Everyday events might have as their consequence a not-so-everyday doom."

Not-so-everyday doom! Yes, excellent. I mean, it's doom, right? What is less everyday than that—and yet what is more possible, given everything?

Unsurprisingly, real extinction events will probably not be the ones of popular imagination. There likely won't be any zombies involved, or Hellmouth expulsions, or even colliding comets. Far more likely are such things as irreversible environmental collapse, heat death, and even now, in these post–Cold War days, nuclear holocaust.

The even more curious conclusion drawn here, as I noted in 1996 and am once again struck by today, is an oxymoronic or at least paradoxical feature of even imagining doom in terms of probability. This, Krieger acknowledged, is because "doom is a transcendent and unique event, and probability concerns the mundane and the potentially repeatable." Thus, "If we construe doom in more mundane nuclear or environmental terms, rather than religious ones, we may find ourselves with the curious conclusion of Kolmogorov—which is, to reiterate, that doom definitely either *will* or *won't* happen, but we *cannot be sure* which. "For when we talk about the path to doom, we are in the scientist's and the historian's realm. And when we talk about an infinite sequence of steps, we are almost surely in the theologian's rather than the scientist's." These warring intellectual approaches will not be easily reconciled, as any sustained reflection on risk shows over and over: faith is forever colliding with mathematics, divinity with determinism.

"But what is perhaps even more curious," Krieger concludes, "is the commitment in both realms to the existence of information. In so far as we are acting on noise, we are in a very different realm indeed."* But wait—what? So we need to separate signal from noise, as always, but the information is lacking in both sacred and mundane accounts of final risk. So then what?

Another philosopher, Nick Bostrom, is most famous for his analysis of the "simulation hypothesis," namely the speculative argument that we are, or must be, living in an elaborate computer program designed by our own far-future, posthuman descendants.† But Bostrom's specialty is what is known as *existential risk*, meaning not the Heideggerian end of my own life but, rather, the prospect of total human extinction. Bostrom urges that

....

* All quotations in this paragraph and in the preceding one are from Krieger, "Could the Probability of Doom Be Zero or One?", 387. For more on information noise as it affects signal and hence prediction, see F. Black, "Noise," in *Business Cycles and Equilibrium* (Cambridge: Blackwell, 1987), 152–72.

† Nick Bostrom, "Are You Living in a Computer Simulation?" *Philosophical Quarterly* 53:211 (2003): 243–55. For those interested, the following rather complex trilemma embraces Bostrom's conclusion to the simulation argument (p. 255):

A technologically mature "posthuman" civilization would have enormous computing power. Based on this empirical fact, the simulation argument shows that at least one of the following propositions is true: (1) The fraction of human-level civilizations that reach a posthuman stage is very close to zero; (2) The fraction of posthuman civilizations that are interested in running ancestor-simulations is very close to zero; (3) The fraction of all people with our kind of experiences that are living in a simulation is very close to one.

If (1) is true, then we will almost certainly go extinct before reaching posthumanity. If (2) is true, then there must be a strong convergence among the courses of advanced civilizations so that virtually none contains any relatively wealthy individuals who desire to run ancestor-simulations and are free to do so. If (3) is true, then we almost certainly live in a simulation. In the dark forest of our current ignorance, it seems sensible to apportion one's credence roughly evenly between (1), (2), and (3).

Unless we are now living in a simulation, our descendants will almost certainly never run an ancestor-simulation.

To which one suitable reaction is, simply, *awesome!*

we distinguish risks along three axes: *scope*, *intensity*, and *probability*. Put simply, scope is extent or degree of reach: personal, local, global. Intensity concerns whether a given risk is endurable or terminal. Probability, Bostrom says, "can be superimposed on the two dimensions."* The following diagram makes the point graphically; category-X risks are the ones that concern human extinction.

Intensity	Endurable	Terminal
Global	Thinning of ozone layer	X
Local	Recession in a country	Genocide
Personal	Car is stolen	Fatal car crash

Scope

Bostrom usefully, and vividly, separates these risks into "bangs" (nuclear holocaust, badly designed machine super-intelligence), "crunches" (resource depletion, eco-system failure), "shrieks" (repressive regimes, bad tech uploads), and "whimpers" (erosive evolution, gradual enslavement by alien overlords). Preventing human extinction is just one of perhaps many goals and moral

* Nick Bostrom, "Existential Risks: Analyzing Human Extinction Scenarios and Related Hazards," *Journal of Evolution and Technology* (March 2002).

imperatives we have, Bostrom says, and so we are driven to the following kind of conclusion: "Since we cannot completely eliminate existential risks (at any moment we could be sent into the dustbin of cosmic history by the advancing front of a vacuum phase transition triggered in a remote galaxy a billion years ago)," he notes, "we should choose the act that has the greatest benefits under the assumption of impending extinction." Some calculations of existential risk imply, by their very uncertainty, "that we should all start partying as if there were no tomorrow. While that option is indisputably attractive, it seems best to acknowledge that there just might be a tomorrow, especially if we play our cards right."

Well, yes. You may conclude philosophy journal articles on a hand-waving point, and that exercise of limbs has its place. Bostrom also offers more practical suggestions than Krieger or some earlier philosophers of doom: the need for more exposure of such risks, the desirability of a workable international framework to negotiate them, above all more critical attention to technological developments in machine learning and non-human intelligence.

We cannot be sanguine out here in what is still laughingly known as the real world, where we have to try to act and create policy right now. Noise is indeed everywhere, as Krieger notes, when we try to assess risks of anything, including human extinction. We must try to cut through it and glean the information useful for our risk calculations. We simply have no choice on that general principle. There is a great deal of choice, and much of it is now exposed as fundamentally political rather than personal. How we conceive and then enact the relevant, always contingent plans of human action can seem an infinite, if not impossible, task.

Thus, it seems to me, we are forcibly returned to where we began, namely, the notion of *risk society* as advanced by Ulrich Beck and others.[*] Risk society is the final and inescapable condition of modernity, conditioned by our technological reliance and too-big-to-fail schemes of getting and spending. This is not likely to change any time soon, and even if it did, we might be worse off than before. Not many people, dedicated anarchists and nihilists aside, are willing to take that particular bet. This does not mean that we must get on board with the house, lean in or buy in or sell out or go all in or any of the other things that capitalist boosters and cheerleaders would have us accept as the only "rational" option.

No, risk assessment is simply a necessary part of risk society. And each of us, as citizens of polities that perforce negotiate risk every day—we could even view our nations and congregations accurately enough as elaborate insurance schemes—has a positive duty to be well-informed and critical about how the social casino is run. This is part of the incurred costs of living together with others, offset by any and all of the personal and collective gains of doing so. This critical responsibility is, if you like, a tax on belonging to something larger than yourself—the politics that, as Aristotle argued, are necessary for all of us who are neither beasts nor gods.

As we have seen, the orders of risk are conceptually distinct but practically related, such that it can be hard to sort out what counts as a right and what counts as a privilege.

....

[*] Cf. note p 55.

And then some people will simply assume that their privileges are rights, sometimes to the point where they can't even recognize them as special benefits not enjoyed by everyone. Or they will make ridiculous choices, confident in the knowledge that there is a family or institutional safety net to catch them when they fall. If we take seriously that there is a birthright lottery, modelled in Rawls's imagined ignorance about who in detail we might be, then some form of egalitarian curb on luck is morally necessary.*

Recognizing the force of these points is simply a matter of good citizenship, whether of a nation or of the world. We can, and should, debate the nuances and the policy implications. But our central duty is, it seems to me, clear. It has been said, perhaps too often, that the only absolutely certain things in life are death and taxes—hence this section's title. The line is typically attributed to Benjamin Franklin, but as is so often the case, that claim would be an unwise bet: Daniel Defoe, who knew a thing or two about plague and risk, got there before Franklin, and Christopher Bullock before him.† In any

----

* There is a vast philosophical literature on what is usually called "luck egalitarianism," with its associated calls for justice schemes that distinguish between responsible choice and brute luck. But as I have tried to show with some examples here, that distinction too is not clean. People suffer as the result of bad luck, and we think they shouldn't have to shoulder bad things that result from what they cannot control; likewise, we often think that they *should* suffer the consequences of bad choices. But these differences can be hard to parse, as indeed can the notions of "suffer," "control," and "consequences."

† Benjamin Franklin, in a 1789 letter to Jean-Baptiste Le Roy: "Our new Constitution is now established, and has an appearance that promises permanency; but in this world nothing can be certain, except death and taxes." Daniel Defoe, in *The Political History of the Devil* (1726): "Things as certain as death and taxes, can be more firmly believ'd." Christopher Bullock, in *The Cobbler of Preston* (1716): "'Tis impossible to be sure of any thing but Death and Taxes." Defoe's *A Journal of the Plague Year* (1722), a semi-fictional account based on events of the (incidentally millennial) 1665 bubonic Great Plague of London, was one of those books, along with Albert Camus's *La Peste* (1947; in English *The Plague*), suddenly enjoying a resurgence of

case, the idiom probably sells taxes a little bit long. One can imagine a life without taxes, and there have been social gatherings that forswore them; but death, at least so far, is the only complete lock bet in life.

Every reviewer's version of a certain quotation in David Foster Wallace's posthumous 2011 novel *The Pale King* attributed the quotation to the fictional Internal Revenue Service employee called DeWitt Glendenning Jr. Each review, like the novel text itself, included the very same square-bracketed addition. The line was this: "The tax code, once you get to know it, embodies all the essence of [human] life: greed, politics, power, goodness, charity."

This trace of bracketing, which seemed odd, sent me on a risky paper chase. Prompted by a fact checker at *Harper's Magazine*, for which I was composing an essay, I laboriously chased down this quotation for several days and eventually found the original in an archived PDF of an old US tax code. It turned out that the philosophical death-and-taxes maxim had been committed to record by a real-life taxman, IRS director Sheldon S. Cohen—but without the "human," which thus stands forever as Wallace's ambiguous, bracketed revision of the original line. The depression-afflicted novelist took his own life in 2008. Talk about death *and* taxes.

* * *

popular interest during the 2020 COVID-19 outbreak.

One could add Giovanni Boccaccio's *Decamerone* (1353; in English *The Decameron*) and Timothy Findley's *Headhunter* (Toronto: HarperCollins, 1993). My favourite treatment of Camus's prophetic novel was Thomas Chatterton Williams, "A Malevolent Holiday," *Harper's Magazine* (June 2020), 7–9, which somehow got exactly right the combinations of disbelief and disregard that characterized the first weeks of the current pandemic, not to mention the strangeness of the coronavirus itself, which is not the Black Death but somehow like it in mystery and global spread.

WHAT IS COMMUNITY as we head into the third decade of the twenty-first century? It is a morass of confusion and contradiction, to be sure, but also still a beacon of hope for a world in which we accommodate not just the robust trees but also the most vulnerable and at-risk ones. This last idea is, after all, the governing norm of the past centuries of nation building, global connection, and international law. We have grown, by difficult stages, more and more inclusive. And while pockets and even systems of exclusion obviously remain—wealth inequality, racial and gender intolerance, colonial and environmental depredation—there is always room left over for hope: what the French philosopher Jacques Derrida memorably defined as "the unresolved remainder" when all daily dialectic had done its sublating work.*

That remainder, the undigested bit of human reason that somehow lies beyond reason, is paradoxically our best chance for future community. It is distinct from optimism, which many experts warned us, in the first months of pandemic lockdown, could be a recipe for anxiety, depression, or bad predictions. Optimism is keyed to the idea of a return to normal, without questioning what I called the darkness of those visions and expectations that dominated the pre-pandemic state of affairs—the *status quo ante* of dream time, in other words.

Optimism is also dangerous if it impairs more existentially inflected forms of coping, because it becomes easy

....

* Derrida discussed hope—sometimes "hope beyond hope"—in a number of sources. A good introduction, which argues (*contra* Richard Rorty) that Derrida's notion of hopeless hope is socially utopian yet nevertheless politically effective, is Mark Dooley, "Private Irony vs. Social Hope: Derrida, Rorty, and the Political," *Cultural Values* 3 (March 2009): 263–90.

prey to disappointment, and hence a dangerous fatalism.*
But then optimism and pessimism become almost indistinguishable judgments on the glass containing half its
volume: Half-full? Half-empty? *Same thing.* Returning to
Leibnizian theodicy for a moment, the philosophical old
joke has it that the optimist believes he is living in the best
of all possible worlds. The pessimist fears that this is true.

And finally, to continue with yet another military
analogy, surviving prisoners of war sometimes describe
how those without optimism had a better chance of
retaining sanity amidst insanity. They did not expect any
kind of return; and that made them especially resilient
to the daily insults and terrors of imprisonment. There
is always a tax on the spirit as well as the body, and the
bank account.

As I was pondering various responses to risks and consequences during the pandemic-dominated weeks of this
writing, I came across an article that felt unlike all the
other things I had been reading, both contemporary and
historical. It was by the writer Julian Brave NoiseCat, of
the Secwepemc/St'at'imc First Nations, called in English
the Interior Squalish people and based in the central and

....

* See, for example, a working paper from the National Bureau of Economic
  Research, "Fatalism, Beliefs, and Behaviors during the COVID-19 Pandemic" (May 2020). The authors note that "individuals dramatically
  overestimate the infectiousness of COVID-19 relative to expert opinion" but
  that "providing people with expert information partially corrects their
  beliefs about the virus." And yet, "the more infectious people believe that
  COVID-19 is, the less willing they are to take social distancing measures, a
  finding we dub the 'fatalism effect.' We estimate that small changes in
  people's beliefs can generate billions of dollars in mortality benefits."
     This behaviour will be familiar to anyone who witnessed the unfolding of
  the 2020 pandemic, but more to the larger point, we can all recognize this
  as quintessential human activity. Soldiers, sailors, and sufferers of mortal
  disease are especially prone to such spasms of fatalism; but we are all its
  potential victims, whenever we abandon hope as we enter the gates of our
  own personal hells.

southern Interior regions of British Columbia, near towns like Kamloops, Chase, D'Arcy, and Lillooet. The essay related how he heard the Blackfoot filmmaker Cowboy Smithx, from southern Alberta, describe Native culture as one composed entirely of "post-apocalyptic people."

What he meant, NoiseCat suggested, was something like this: "As Indians, I think we've been told that we're supposed to be dead and gone so many times that we've internalized it. Some of us don't want to be anymore. In a society built atop our graves, survival has become an act of resistance." And further, it meant this: "We've inherited a vision so audacious, it terrified our oppressors. It's a worldview that celebrates beauty, defiance, and a playful wagging of the finger at the people who tried to kill us. After the pandemic but as the climate crisis unfolds, maybe more people will understand what it means to survive and still dream, like us."*

The last comment followed hard on details of how L. Frank Baum, beloved creator of *The Wonderful Wizard of Oz* (1900), had written an editorial in the *Aberdeen Saturday Pioneer* a week after the December 29, 1890, massacre and mass burial of Lakota ghost dancers by the United States military. The editorial included this genocidal injunction: "Our only safety depends upon the total extermination of the Indians. Having wronged them for centuries we had better, in order to protect our civilization, follow it up by one more wrong and wipe these untamed and untameable creatures from the face of the

....

* Julian Brave NoiseCat, "How to Survive an Apocalypse and Keep Dreaming," *Nation*, June 2, 2020. NoiseCat also relates Cowboy Smithx's plan to purchase Castle Calgary in Scotland and rename it *mohkínstsis*, which means "elbow"—the original Blackfoot name for Calgary, Alberta, where the Bow River bends. This is what Smithx labels "inverted colonialism."

earth." Which is the kind of double-down logic all too common in our own day, 130 years later.

What is it to be *post-apocalyptic*? Well, it is not to entertain the usual play of utopian and dystopian options so often found in speculative fiction and CGI-heavy films, illuminating or entertaining though those may often be. Too often, that binary division in imaginative rendering of life after apocalypse collapses into a futile and meaningless simulacrum of dialectic thought—usually executed, yes, with lots of expensive cinematic special effects. Rather, to be post-apocalyptic is to contemplate the total destruction of one's culture *even when* one's life continues. And then it is to witness, without apology and often with hypocritical "anti-racist" virtue signalling, the names and images of that culture repurposed as sports logos or gas station signs or trade names for butter and syrup—also football, hockey, and baseball.[*]

....

[*] In the wake of anti–Black racism protests over the killing of George Floyd, celebrities and corporations rushed to embrace the suddenly acceptable, even trendy, position of protest and Black Lives Matter (as if they hadn't all along). The resulting Twitter meme known as "This you?" mocked this self-serving move by lining up past racists acts, campaigns, or features of the would-be social justice warriors.

It is easy, and maybe fun, to mock posturing actors and musicians as presumptive trend-chasing dummies. Large corporations are another matter. My personal favourite "this you" response ran next to the Washington NFL team's smug #BlackOutTuesday tweet—a blacked-out screen—and featured a full-colour reproduction of the team's "Indian head" logo, without any further comment. The franchise owners had consistently refused to alter the logo or the derogatory team name, as has the Cleveland major-league baseball team, whose nickname dates from 1915. The Washington owners argue, outrageously, that their franchise name, adopted in 1913, honours Indigenous people.

Responding to calls for more proactive racial sensitivity, Quaker Oats, owners of the 131-year-old Aunt Jemima syrup brand, promised to remove the highly offensive happy-mamma-cook image and name from the product. This decision rightly provoked further calls to change or eliminate Uncle Ben's rice, Land O'Lakes butter, and Mrs. Butterworth's rival syrup. The NFL team in Washington, the baseball team in Cleveland, and the Canadian Football League franchise in Edmonton were also on the docket. See Angela R. Riley and Sonia

To survive and still to dream. This is to imagine beyond optimism, to transcend possibility and probability both, after the manner of what Jonathan Lear, writing of the destruction of the American Crow people, called "radical hope."*

Like most people who enjoy relative privilege and comfort, living in my own fragile corner of the house of cards, I don't really know what that feels like. But I try to make sense of it, as we watch the world turned upside down, becoming a warren of risk and attendant injustices. I want, like so many of us, to believe in an audacious vision. But maybe we have to survive apocalypse before we can even dream that transcendent dream.

We are not yet prisoners of war, just of circumstance. We are not yet victims of military massacre, though the prospect is continually held in reserve, at the ready. We want to be survivors, but only if we can be together. Hope limns the contours of community, now and always. Tax schemes are perhaps inevitable, but if so, they need to be at least minimally equitable. Estate and inheritance tax curb, if they cannot completely eliminate, the structural harms and benefits of the massively unfair birthright lottery. Graduated income tax works to enable some limited

....

K. Katyal, "Aunt Jemima Is Gone. Can We Finally End All Racist Branding?" *New York Times*, June 19, 2020. By mid-2020, both the Washington and Edmonton football teams had announced they would change names—though in the former case only after sustained pressure from corporate partners.

* Jonathan Lear, *Radical Hope: Ethics in the Face of Cultural Devastation* (Cambridge, MA: Harvard University Press, 2008). In this book Lear concentrates on Plenty Coups, the last great Chief of the Crow Nation, who related to the white philosopher the story of his people—up to a certain point. "When the buffalo went away the hearts of my people fell to the ground," he said, "and they could not lift them up again. After this nothing happened." This notion of *nothing happened after* is central to the radical nature of hope: normal events are suspended; there are no events; time is stopped or simply over. And yet life, or at least survival, goes on.

version of John Rawls's maxim in principle, such that the gains of the very well off are never scored at the expense of, only with a summed benefit to, the least well off. You can always get ahead; but others should not fall behind because of that. Rawls called this, as noted earlier, *justice as fairness*. Can we imagine a just society that is at least a fair society, if not an ideal one? I think we can. I likewise think that feeling post-apocalyptic might turn out to be the arc of hope that bends towards that end. A more just and equitable world is possible. This is our time, this is our place, to make that happen.

Here is what we can do:

Insist on drastically reformed taxation schemes that actually approach some reasonable notion of fairness. Begin real conversations about reparations and structural corrections for identifiable groups who have suffered from systematic overexposure to risk. Enable compensation programs beyond mere payer-run insurance plans or corrupt government relief organizations for the victims of disaster, whether sudden or long-term. Regulate social media strictly and consistently to reduce the stress level of everyday life, including presidential tirades and targeted takedowns of other people.

Enact a universal basic income to buffer market failures and random job loss. Crack down on private equity and other predatory financial industries, otherwise known as carving profit out of other people's misfortune.

If we wanted to go further, how about no more corporate bailouts at the expense of ordinary stakeholders. No more opacity, lying, cronyism, and bogus apologies in governance. No more smiling and log rolling between business and politics.

These are dreams, yes. But we are in a different kind of dream time now: not the privileged delusions of merit and security enjoyed by the lucky few, but rather the open space of possibility created by shared existential threat. Sometimes dreams become realities, but only if they are entertained, experienced with force, taken seriously. The traditional eulogy in the Anglican tradition is a familiar saying: "In the midst of death, we are in life." This life-affirming sentiment, the ultimate *memento mori*, actually inverts a long-standing line from a medieval Gregorian chant: *Media vita in morte sumus*—"In the midst of life, we are in death."* The inversion says the same thing as the original, though, and that is both amazing and bracing. Life goes on even as death is a daily reality. As the common Latin tag has it, for example as written on a human skull in Charles Ryder's *Brideshead Revisited* Oxford rooms: *Et in Arcadia Ego*. "I, too, am in Paradise." Mortality always claims its place, even in a bucolic idyll.†

I have seen many people say, in these lengthening days of lockdown, rising death tolls, and pervasive economic fear and anxiety, that *hope is not a plan*. And yet the right kind of hope might just be the best plan we could ever fashion. Some months into the pandemic, thoughtful writers seemed to rediscover the power of hope—*calloused* hope, as one political figure called it, noting that this was neither cheap nor easy.‡ And then, I would add,

....

* Rite Two of the Memorial Service, *Book of Common Prayer.*

† The Latin formulation has been used in numerous works of art and literature, from paintings by Poussin (1637–38) and Guercino (c. 1618–22) to episodes of *Star Trek: Picard* (2020). Puzzle-freaks and Dan Brown fans have noted that it is an anagram of another Latin phrase, *I Tegro Arcana Dei*, which translates as "Begone, I conceal the secrets of God." Well, why not?

‡ Cory Booker, quoted in Nicholas Kristof, "We Interrupt This Gloom to

when your calloused hands get to work out of recognition of bleakness and catastrophe, hope becomes *radical*.

As noted from the beginning, any consideration of risk has been decisively altered by the current conditions of pandemic, racial conflict, and economic distress. These conditions are neither unprecedented nor final. One theme of this book has been that we can never entirely eliminate risk in life, even if we wanted to. Another has been that risk is always political, even while seeming random and fixed. And so a third has been that risk can be, at least partly, assessed and managed. We can't change the first point. But we can act to improve the third by insisting on the second.

Bet on that, friends, with some post-apocalyptic political hope coiled into your next roll of the dice or spin of the wheel. We can, and we must, do better in future. Every bet, in games both mortal and trivial, is an action performed in the present under the temporal dome of future outcomes. That relentless series of time-based bargains, the hard conditions of all assumed risk, defines the horizon of meaning in the world. As Pascal said of his own mortal Wager, you must bet because you are already embarked.

Les jeux sont faits.

Offer ... Hope," *New York Times*, July 16, 2020.

Acknowledgements

MY THANKS TO Dan Wells of Biblioasis, who has been interested in thoughts about risk and the idea of a "field notes" pamphlet series for some time. This book is the result of that conjunction.

Thanks to Tatum Hands at LA+ magazine, where a section of the current book first appeared in a special issue on "Risk" (Fall 2017, pp. 6–11). Another section appears, in different form, in the LA+ special issue on "Community" (Spring 2021).

I am grateful to Andrew Potter, Benjamin Davis, Natasha Hassan, Molly Montgomery, and Katherine Crone for various kinds of help and inspiration.

This book is dedicated to my father, Joseph Arthur Gerald Kingwell (Flt. Lt./Capt., RCAF-CAF, ret.), who was sometimes a risk-taker but never a gambler.

MARK KINGWELL is Professor of Philosophy at the University of Toronto and a contributing editor of *Harper's Magazine*, and has written for publications ranging from *Adbusters* and the *New York Times* to the *Journal of Philosophy* and *Auto Racing Digest*. Among his twenty books of political and cultural theory are the national best-sellers *Better Living*, *The World We Want*, and *Glenn Gould*. In order to secure financing for their continued indulgence he has also written about his various hobbies, including fishing, baseball, cocktails, and contemporary art. His most recent book is *Wish I Were Here: Boredom and the Interface* (McGill-Queen's University Press, 2019), which won the 2020 Erving Goffman Award for scholarship in media ecology.